The Ombudsman:

Twenty-Five Years On

The Ombudsman: Twenty-Five Years On

A Series of Conference Papers
presented at
Leicester Polytechnic
March 1992

Edited by

Professor Neil Hawke

De Montfort University Leicester

De Montfort University Law Monographs

Cavendish Publishing Limited

First published in Great Britain 1993 by Cavendish Publishing Limited,
23A Countess Road, London NW5 2XH.
Telephone: 071-485 0303 Facsimile: 071-485 0304

British Library Cataloguing in Publication Data

The Ombudsman: Twenty-Five Years On
(De Montfort University Law Monographs)
I Series
354.410091

ISBN 1-874241-17-1

Printed and bound in Great Britain

The Contributors

Professor Roy Gregory is Professor of Politics and a member of the Centre for Ombudsman Studies at the University of Reading.

Jane Pearson is a Research Fellow and member of the Centre for Ombudsman Studies at the University of Reading.

Professor Mick Ryan is Professor of Government at the University of Greenwich.

Tony Ward is lecturer in Law at the Department of Law, De Montfort University Law School, Leicester.

Professor Howard Elcock is Professor of Government at the University of Northumbria, Newcastle.

Elizabeth Hodder is County Ombudsperson, Bedfordshire County Council.

F G Laws is Vice Chairman, Commission for Local Administration in England.

Introduction

This series of papers was presented at a conference held in 1992 to mark the twenty-fifth anniversary of the creation of a first 'national' Ombudsman under the Parliamentary Commissioner Act 1967. The distinguished contributors present an intriguing picture of Ombudsmen in a number of contexts. Gregory and Pearson chart the issues of accessibility to the Parliamentary Commissioner emphasising the significant relationship with members of Parliament. Ryan and Ward introduce a particularly contemporary theme with an analysis of the arguments surrounding very recent proposals for a so-called 'Prison Ombudsman'. A comparative dimension is introduced with an examination of the Polish Commissioner for Civil Rights Protection in the paper by Elcock. A significant element of the paper is the issue of competence to deal with the legality of administrative action, an enduring controversy in relation to the Parliamentary Commissioner's jurisdiction in this country. The matter is returned to in the paper by Laws on the Local Government Ombudsman, a paper indicating a range of dynamics that continue to shape the Ombudsman remedy. The fact that the Ombudsman remedy is still very much a 'live' topic in local government can be seen in the paper by Hodder on the relatively recent Bedfordshire Ombudsperson scheme.

Professor Neil Hawke

Contents

Chapter 1

The Parliamentary Ombudsman after twenty-five years: Problems and solutions

Roy Gregory and Jane Pearson

I

The Ombudsman arrangements which came into effect in the United Kingdom on 1 April 1967 got off to a bad start. As one observer notes, few governmental agencies can have begun work under 'a darker cloud of adverse publicity' than did the Parliamentary Commissioner for Administration.[1] The new Office was denounced as 'pointless', 'a joke', 'a gimmick' and 'ludicrously emasculated'. The first Commissioner himself was variously described by the media and in Parliament as a 'toothless tiger'; 'a watchdog in chains'; 'a swordless crusader'; an 'ombudsflop'; an 'ombudsboob'; and an 'ombudsmouse'.[2] To some extent, such expressions of disappointment merely reflected the vague and unrealistic notions of ill-informed critics labouring under the mistaken impression that, in other countries, virtually nothing was beyond the powers of review and direction vested in the Ombudsman. The fact that no Ombudsman properly so described is anywhere authorised to make orders, reverse administrative action, or enforce remedies, was sometimes ignored in the chorus of disapproval and derision.[3]

Not all the criticisms levelled at the Parliamentary Commissioner scheme, however, were based upon ignorance of the Ombudsman concept. It was not unreasonable to argue complainants should have been given direct access to the Commissioner, instead of being required to ask MPs to refer their cases to the Office; or that his jurisdiction was too restricted, in the sense that the Office was empowered to investigate only administrative action taken by central government departments, and not even all of that; or that the inclusion of the term 'maladministration' in the Parliamentary Commissioner Act 1967 had been ill-considered, because it both unduly restricted the range and number of complaints open to investigation by the Commissioner and also limited unduly the grounds on which he was authorised to criticise departmental action subject to complaint.

1 See William B Gwyn, 'The Ombudsman in Britain: a Qualified Success in Government Reform', *Public Administration*, Summer 1982.

2 See William B Gwyn, 'The British PCA: Ombudsman of Ombudsmouse?', *Journal of Politics*, February 1973.

3 For the characteristics, functions and powers of Ombudsman institutions, see DC Rowat 'The Ombudsman. Citizen's Defender' (Allen and Unwin, 1968); and Gerald E Caiden and Niall MacDermot, 'The Institution of Ombudsman' in Gerald E Caiden (ed), *International Handbook of the Ombudsman. Evolution and Present Function* (Greenwood Press, 1983).

In addition to what sceptics regarded as design faults of this kind, incorporated in the original legislation, other features of the Parliamentary Commissioner scheme also came under attack as it took shape. The government had been wrong, it was argued, to appoint a former civil servant to the post of Parliamentary Commissioner. The first Commissioner was said to have interpreted the term 'maladministration' too cautiously. It was undesirable that the Office should be staffed with what were described as 'junior' civil servants, seconded from the very departments they were responsible for investigating. The lack of legal expertise in the Office was deplorable. All in all, the Parliamentary Commissioner scheme as portrayed by its detractors amounted to a largely worthless variant of the Ombudsman model, unlikely to do much good, if indeed it had any future at all.[4]

A decade later the Parliamentary Commissioner scheme was still the subject of criticism. The arrangements for access to the Office through MPs; the restrictions on the Commissioner's jurisdiction; and the 'maladministration provisions' in the 1967 Act were still thought to be undesirable.[5] By 1977, however, there was favourable comment, too. Not only had the Commissioner carried out 'a number of important and successful investigations'; the Office, it was acknowledged, had become established and accepted 'as a permanent part of the constitution'. Indeed, in an oblique tribute to the effectiveness of the Office on those occasions when it did come into play, criticism of the Parliamentary Commissioner scheme began to take a rather different turn. The problem (critics now argued) was that the Parliamentary Commissioner scheme was not well enough publicised; it was not widely known to the public; it was employed by only a small section of the population; and therefore was 'considerably under-utilised'.[6]

As the Parliamentary Commissioner scheme approaches the twenty-fifth anniversary of its inception, it continues to provoke mixed feelings. On the other hand, the value of the Office and its associated Select Committee is clearly accepted beyond question. In evidence to the Select Committee in December 1989 the then Leader of the House agreed that 'the system' was working well[7]; and the Select Committee, in its Report published in December 1990, expressed the view that the Parliamentary Commissioner scheme was now 'part of the fabric of the United Kingdom's unwritten constitution'.[8] On the occasion of a rare debate on the work of the Office on 1 May 1991 there was a general agreement among MPs present that 'the Ombudsman system'

4 See Roy Gregory and Peter Hutchesson, *The Parliamentary Ombudsman. A Study in the Control of Administrative Action* (Allen and Unwin, 1975), pp.619-20.

5 See JUSTICE, *Our Fettered Ombudsman* (Justice, 1977).

6 *Ibid*, pp.3-4.

7 See *Select Committee*, Minutes of Evidence, 5 December 1989, QQ 14-16.

8 See *First Report from the Select Committee, 1990-91*, H.C. 129, 19 December 1990, p.xiii.

had been on the whole a 'success story'.[9] And at a Select Committee hearing in December 1991 it was again made clear that the Government, too, regarded the role of the Commissioner and the way in which it had been discharged as 'a very considerable success', something to be enhanced, and certainly not diminished.[10]

Indeed, the Parliamentary Commissioner scheme is now praised, in moderation, even by journalists, lawyers and academics. The Commissioner's investigations, it is pointed out, are extremely thorough; he has made officials aware of the need to treat members of the public with proper consideration; government departments have frequently provided remedies in response to his findings; administrative practice and policy (and even, on occasion, the law) has been changed, to the benefit of thousands, as a result of his operations and those of the Select Committee; and his reports have helped complainants secure redress which they would almost certainly have been denied had the Office not existed. All of this, it is pointed out, has been accomplished without damaging civil service morale or significantly increasing departmental workloads. Nor has the doctrine of Ministerial accountability to Parliament been undermined. If the United Kingdom ever seriously addresses itself to the question of administrative law reform, it is suggested, a primary source of information will be the reports of the Parliamentary Commissioner.[11]

On the other hand, by no means every observer is persuaded that the full potential of the Office has yet been realised. It is not so much that the watchdog is thought to lack teeth; the feeling is, rather, that he is too infrequently asked to make use of them. Even the Select Committee, for the most part content with the way in which Parliamentary Commissioner scheme has developed, suggests that 'the current system would be strengthened if references were made by more MPs'.[12] In short, as the authors of one recent analysis of the Parliamentary Commissioner scheme conclude, the Office is 'capable of better things'.[13]

Reservations of this kind are prompted in the main by statistics. The number of 'justified' complaints upheld by the Commissioner is, of course, related to the number of cases investigated; which, in turn, is related to the number of cases falling within the Commissioner's jurisdiction, referred to him by MPs. The figures are set out in Tables 1 and 2 (see pages 4 and 5).

9 See H.C. deb., 1990-91, 190, cols.367-405.

10 See *Second Report from the Select Committee, 1991-92,* (The Implications of the Citizen's Charter for the Work of the Parliamentary Commissioner for Administration) H.C. 158, 5 February 1992, Minutes of Evidence, 18 December 1991, Q.63.

11 See Stanley de Smith and Rodney Brazier, *Constitutional and Administrative Law* (Penguin Books, 6th edn., 1989), pp.653-4; for other examples, see P Birkinshaw, *Grievances, Remedies and the State* (Sweet and Maxwell, 1985), pp.139-40; HWR Wade, *Administrative Law* (Clarendon Press, 1988), pp.94-5; and B L Jones, *Garner's Administrative Law* (Butterworths, 1989), p.104.

12 See *Report from the Select Committee, 1990-91,* 19 December 1990, p.xii.

13 See Gavin Drewry and Carol Harlow, 'A 'Cutting Edge'? The Parliamentary Commissioner and MPs, *Modern Law Review*, 53, 6 November 1990.

Table 1

Complaints upheld by the Parliamentary Commissioner

	Complaints investigated	Complaints upheld	Percentage
1967	188	19	10.1
1968	374	38	10.2
1969	302	48	15.9
1970	259	59	22.8
1971	182	67	36.8
1972	261	79	30.3
1973	239	88	36.8
1974	252	94	37.3
1975	244	90	36.9
1976	320	139	43.4
1977	312	111	35.6
1978	341	131	38.4
1979	223	84	37.7
1980	225	107	47.6
1981	228	104	45.6
1982	202	67	33.2
1983	198	83	41.9
1984	183	81	44.3
1985	177	75	42.4
1986	168	82	48.8
1987	145	63	43.5
1988	120	59	49.2
1989	126	61	48.4
1990	177	74	41.8

SOURCE: Parliamentary Commissioner: *Annual Reports*

Table 2

Cases referred to the Parliamentary Commissioner

	Complaints received direct from public	Number of MPs referring cases	Cases referred by MPs	Complaints rejected as outwith Jurisdiction	Percentage of cases rejected
1967	743	428	1,069	561	52.5
1968	808	N/A	1,120	727	64.9
1969	814	N/A	761	445	58.5
1970	645	N/A	645	362	56.1
1971	505	305	548	295	53.8
1972	661	306	573	318	55.5
1973	676	306	571	285	49.9
1974	724	359	704	374	53.1
1975	1,068	381	928	576	62.1
1976	882	375	815	492	60.4
1977	868	401	901	504	55.9
1978	1,777	461	1,259	927	73.6
1979	822	368	758	541	71.4
1980	1,194	401	1,031	686	66.5
1981	870	387	917	694	75.7
1982	1,002	389	838	574	68.5
1983	952	462	751	605	80.6
1984	901	386	837	658	78.6
1985	935	373	759	606	79.8
1986	838	387	719	549	76.4
1987	1,097	379	677	509	75.2
1988	1,132	359	701	529	75.5
1989	1,012	361	677	502	74.2
1990	1,039	371	704	535	76.0

SOURCE: Parliamentary Commissioner: *Annual Reports*

For what averages are worth, the yearly average number of cases investigated in the period 1967 to 1990 was 227; the yearly average number of complaints referred by MPs was 803. These numbers have always been regarded and described as 'low', the implication being that, ideally, they 'ought' to have been higher.

It is indeed true that in countries with populations a great deal smaller than that of the United Kingdom the Ombudsman sometimes receives and investigates far more cases than does the Parliamentary Commissioner. In 1990, for example, the Danish Ombudsman was expected to receive more than 2,000 complaints from a population of around five million. The Swedish Ombudsman expected to receive about 4,000 case in the same Year from a population of eight million. These figures are in marked contrast to the 766 complaints which the Commissioner received in 1989 from the United Kingdom population of over 55 million.[14]

Unqualified statistics, however should be treated with caution. The jurisdictional remits of Ombudsmen vary considerably from one country to another, and in some they are a good deal more extensive than that of the Parliamentary Commissioner. In Sweden, for example, the Ombudsman's jurisdiction covers not only state servants in the conventional sense but also the actions of the courts of law and priests of the Church of Sweden. Moreover, in countries like Sweden and Denmark, where (it seems) he is often the aggrieved person's first and only port of call outside of the organisation concerned, the Ombudsman naturally receives more complaints than are referred to the Parliamentary Commissioner in a country such as the United Kingdom, where MPs have always played a major role in taking up constituents' grievances against governmental agencies.[15]

The fact is that in a country like the United Kingdom, with its large population and long-established tradition of employing MPs as 'constituency grievance men', it can certainly be argued that the Commissioner 'ought' to investigate 'only complaints that the Member has been, or knows that he will be, unable to resolve himself'.[16] Looked at in that light, the number of cases referred each year to the Office is not perhaps as spectacularly low as may at first sight appear. This is not to say, however, that it is necessarily the 'right' number. Ideally, the Commissioner would receive and investigate only and *all* those complaints which MPs have been, or know that they will be, unable to resolve themselves. How many such cases there are, no one knows.

What can be said with certainty is that the Parliamentary Commissioner's case-load is remarkably light by comparison with the number of cases taken

14 See *First Report from the Select Committee, 1990-91,* p.xii.

15 *Ibid*, pp.v-iv.

16 *Ibid*, p.xii citing *Fourth Report from the Select Committee, 1977-78* (Review of Access and Jurisdiction), H.C. 615 and 444, 26 July 1978, p.vii.

up by members of the public with their MPs. During the debates on the Parliamentary Commissioner Bill in 1967 it was estimated that, between them, MPs received about 300,000 complaints a year.[17] The Commissioner's case-load is also remarkably light by comparison with the number of cases pursued by MPs with Ministers. In the early 1960s it was suggested that 'upwards of 50,000 letters a year' passed between MPs and Ministers.[18] In 1976 it was reported that the DHSS alone was dealing with about 25,000 letters a year from MPs to Ministers.[19] At much the same time, in 1978, the then Parliamentary Commissioner estimated that there were about 200,000 'contacts' a year between MPs and major departments, 100,000 of which involved letters.[20] Not all of these letters deal with complaints; and not all complaints pursued by MPs with Ministers are investigatable by the Commissioner. None the less the difference between the number of complaints received and taken up by MPs on the one hand, and the number of cases which, between them, they refer to the Parliamentary Commissioner every year, does remain strikingly large.

Equally striking, perhaps, are the same figures for referrals looked at in terms of the number of cases per constituency reaching the Commissioner. As Table 3 (see page 8) shows, in 1986 the constituencies represented by some 463 MPs generated altogether only 200 complaints for the Commissioner's attention. The millions of constituents represented by 263 Members evidently produced *no complaints at all* for investigation by the Office. Every year, as Table 2 indicates, there have been many constituencies from which the Commissioner has received not a single case. They have not necessarily been the same constituencies from year to year, of course. Even so, in May 1974 the Commissioner revealed that over the lifetime of the 1970-74 Parliament 'something over 120' Members had not referred even one case to him.[21]

Figures like these cannot, of course, be said to 'prove' that the Parliamentary Commissioner scheme is under-used. It may be, as the Select Committee judiciously observed in July 1978, that all the MPs who had not referred a single complaint to the Office since October 1974 had dealt with their constituency cases so efficiently that there had been no need for them to seek the Commissioner's assistance. On the other hand, the Select Committee suggested, it was also possible that some at least of these Members had not

17 See H.C. Deb., 1966-67, 734, col.89.

18 See D N Chester and Nona Bowring, *Questions in Parliament* (Clarendon Press, 1962), p.104

19 See M Hartley-Brewer, 'The importance of being a good constituency man', *The Guardian*, 17 September 1976.

20 See *Third Report from the Select Committee*, H.C. 544, 1978, p.3. The latter figure was subsequently endorsed by the Civil Service Department; see *Fourth Report from the Select Committee, 1977-78,* p.vii.

21 See *Report from the Select Committee, 1974* H.C. 268, 17 July 1974, Minutes of Evidence, 8 May 1974, Q.1.

Table 3

Number of MPs referring cases to the Parliamentary Commissioner: 1986

Number of MPs referring cases	Percentage of MPs referring cases	No of cases referred
263	40.5	0
200	51.7	1
102	26.4	2
43	11.1	3
30	7.8	4
7	1.8	5
4	-	6
1	-	7

SOURCE: Drewry and Harlow (1990)

fully appreciated the role the Commissioner could play.[22] More than a decade later little had changed. Describing itself as 'somewhat concerned' to hear that in 1989 only 361 MPs had used the services of the Commissioner, in December 1990 the Select Committee reported that it 'suspected' that some MPs were not using the Office because of a 'lack of knowledge of his exact role and powers'.[23]

As we will see in Part II of this paper, MPs' 'lack of knowledge', though no doubt an important consideration, is probably not the only explanation of the relatively small number of cases referred to the Commissioner. What needs to be done, or at least considered, in order to overcome this problem is discussed in Part III.

II

It is often pointed out that the extent to which an Ombudsman system is used is very much in the hands of the general public. How much use the citizen makes of an Ombudsman is, in turn, related to the degree of public awareness of his existence and functions.[24] To what extent the relatively small number of cases handled by the Parliamentary Commissioner can be attributed to ignorance of the Office we simply do not know, although survey evidence about the public awareness of other Ombudsman arrangements suggests that much of the population probably knows little or nothing about the Commissioner or his work.[25]

The citizen's awareness of an Ombudsman system, however, is not the only consideration which affects the degree to which it is used. The arrangements for gaining access to it may also help determine the number of cases an Ombudsman institution investigates. As with the French Mediateur, access to the Parliamentary Commissioner is of course indirect. Only MPs may refer complaints to the Office for investigation. This feature of the Parliamentary Commissioner scheme ensures that the extent to which the Office is employed is a matter not only for the general public, but is also very much under the control of MPs.

When constituents take the initiative and ask MPs to refer complaints to the Commissioner, they may react in a variety of ways. They may agree to pass on the case immediately, without more ado. They may resort to the Commissioner

22 See *Fourth Report from the Select Committee, 1977-78,* p.x.

23 See *First Report from the Select Committee, 1990-91,* H.C. 129, 19 December 1990, p.xii.

24 See, for example, Gerald E Caiden and Niall MacDermot, loc.cit., p.6; and *Fourth Report from the Select Committee, 1990-91,* H.C. 368, 10 July 1991, p.vi.

25 The *Annual Consumer Dissatisfaction Survey 1990* showed that when prompted 27 per cent of consumers were aware of the Insurance Ombudsman, 24 per cent of the Banking Ombudsman and 22 per cent of the Building Societies Ombudsman. As the survey notes, these figures are almost certainly over-estimates. See Office of Fair Trading, *Consumer Redress,* November 1991, p.57.

only when other methods of securing redress have been tried without success. Use of the Parliamentary Commissioner scheme may at any stage be discouraged by MPs who are unfamiliar with the functions of the Office or have no confidence in it. Faced with an insistent complainant few MPs may be prepared gratuitously to risk giving offence to a constituent by flatly refusing to pass on his case, unless of course they are sure that it is outwith the Commissioner's jurisdiction. The fact remains, however, that in principle it is open to MPs to decline to refer complaints for any or no reason at all.

A sequence of this kind, with aggrieved persons taking the initiative in asking MPs to refer cases to the Office, was clearly one of the scenarios which Government spokesmen and back-benchers alike had in mind when the Parliamentary Commissioner scheme was under discussion in the mid-1960s. Members were told that they should not overload the Office by making complaints indiscriminately, so that the Commissioner had to waste his time 'sifting out nothing but chaff'. If the scheme was to work, the Government argued, MPs would have to do the initial 'filtering'. MPs would themselves (it was hoped) act as a 'screen' for a lot of complaints which could be better dealt with by other methods when they were sure that a particular complaint was not an appropriate one for the Commissioner, or when they considered that it was a case which they could take up more effectively and expeditiously with the Minister. After all, it was pointed out, it would probably take longer for the Office to investigate a case than it would for a Member to deal with it in one of the traditional ways.[26]

Implicit in the Government's description of the Parliamentary Commissioner scheme, however, there was also another, rather different scenario. The Office was described as 'a wholly Parliamentary institution', designed to help MPs carry out their traditional functions on behalf of constituents. The Government's objective, it was explained, was to give MPs a 'better instrument' with which to protect the citizen. Providing the back-bench MP with 'a new and powerful weapon with a sharp cutting-edge to be added to the antiquated armoury of Parliamentary questions and adjournment debates', the Commissioner's investigations would make available the possibility of a thorough and impartial investigation into alleged maladministration. The knowledge that this 'new servant of the House' was there should surely put heart into back-benchers who felt that they counted for little more than lobby fodder. Through the Office of the Parliamentary Commissioner, it was said, the Government was putting at the disposal of the back-bench MP 'an extremely sharp and piercing instrument of investigation'.[27]

26 See H.C. Deb., 1966-67,734, col.61; and Standing Committee B, 3 November 1966, cols.130-1, 165-6.

27 See *The Parliamentary Commissioner for Administration*, Cmnd. 2767, 1965; and H.C. Deb., 1966-67, 734, cols.44, 49 and 60.

The fact is, of course, that 'instruments' and 'servants' are by definition at the disposal of owners and masters to be employed as and when the latter think fit. When MPs use the 'antiquated armoury' of Parliamentary questions and adjournment debates they do so of their own volition, and not because aggrieved constituents have requested them to deal with their complaints by means of any particular Parliamentary or informal method of securing redress. In other words, in this second model of the Parliamentary Commissioner scheme at work it was evidently envisaged that, even when aggrieved constituents had never even heard of the Parliamentary Commissioner, it would be perfectly natural for MPs, given the complainant's consent, themselves to take the initiative in referring cases to the Office.

How often MPs do in fact take it upon themselves to suggest that complaints should be referred to the Commissioner we do not know. Pointing out that even those constituents who have some idea of what an Ombudsman is and does may not recognise the 'Commissioner' terminology, one observer suggests that if they approach a Member with a complaint they may well fail to ask him to pass it on to the Commissioner.

He continues:

> 'Since MPs are overburdened by correspondence, and have been estimated to write some hundred thousand letters annually to departments, it seems unlikely that all invariably trouble themselves further by inquiring of constituents whether they wish the Commissioner to act.'[28]

No more, it may be supposed, would MPs enquire of complainants who have no idea of what an Ombudsman is or does - almost certainly a considerably larger category - whether they wish their cases to go to the Commissioner.

As both 'gatekeepers' (keeping out and letting in complaints from people who know about the Office and wish to use it) and 'magnets' (attracting to themselves complaints from constituents who are unaware of the Parliamentary Commissioner's existence and passing on some of these cases to the Office), MPs are thus in a position very largely to determine the extent to which the Parliamentary Commissioner scheme is utilised.

Confirming what is obvious enough from the official statistics, Table 4 (see page 12) indicates that in the very early years of the Parliamentary Commissioner scheme MPs were making use of the Office far less frequently than they employed other techniques for seeking the redress of constituents' grievances. In a survey of MPs conducted in 1970, whereas 100 per cent of MPs reported that it was their practice to write to the Minister 'often, very

28 See Kenneth P Poole, 'United Kingdom' in Gerald E Caiden (ed), op.cit., p.198.

Table 4

Comparative Frequency of Usage of Parliamentary Techniques for Seeking Redress of Grievances (percentages of MPs)

	Parliamentary Techniques				
Frequency of usage	**PCA**	**Parliamentary Question**	**Approach Official**	**Talk to Minister**	**Letter to Minister**
Never	10.9	4.3	18.2	0.7	-
Very rarely, rarely	80.8	60.0	27.3	52.7	-
Often, very often	8.3	35.7	46.9	45.9	67.6
Always	-	-	7.6	0.7	32.5
Totals	100.0	100.0	100.0	100.0	100.0

SOURCE: Gregory and Alexander (1973)

often or always', over 90 per cent of the Members questioned said that they resorted to the Commissioner 'rarely, very rarely, or never'.[29]

The propensity of MPs to make use of the Office, it seems reasonable to assume, is related in turn to their views as to its usefulness for their purposes. When asked to assess the utility of the various informal and Parliamentary techniques available to them for securing the redress of constituents' grievances, as Table 5 (see page 14) shows, the rating 'moderately effective, effective or highly effective' was given to Parliamentary Questions by 58.5 per cent of Members; to adjournment debates by 66.5 per cent of Members; and to letters to Ministers by 92.2 per cent of Members. By contrast only 41.6 per cent of MPs thought that the Parliamentary Commissioner was equally effective. And whereas the rating 'somewhat ineffective, ineffective or highly effective' was given to Parliamentary Questions by 22.1 per cent of Members; to adjournment debates by 16.9 per cent of Members; and to letters to Ministers by 1.3 per cent of respondents, as many as 29.9 per cent of Members gave this negative evaluation to the Parliamentary Commissioner.[30]

As to why MPs judged the Office to be comparatively ineffective and used it relatively infrequently in the late 1960s, there appeared to be two possible explanations. First, there was the question of dispatch. If a constituent's grievance was redressed as a result of a Member's efforts on his behalf the remedy was likely to be forthcoming far more quickly following a letter to the Minister than after a reference to the Commissioner. Because the Parliamentary Commissioner's investigations were nothing if not through, they were likely also to be lengthy operations, the average time required to dispose of a case (in the late 1960s) being about five months. Some of the more complex cases, it was noted, took a great deal longer. Clearly, in terms of rapid results the Office could not compete with alternative methods of seeking the redress of grievances.

Second, MPs' replies to the 1970 survey left little room for doubt that their lukewarm response to the Parliamentary Commissioner scheme related less to the quality of his work when he was able to help them than to dissatisfaction with the fact that he was unable to help them more often and over a wider field of public administration. Asked to say which aspects of the Parliamentary Commissioner scheme they considered inadequate, 72 per cent of MPs surveyed mentioned as their first response the restriction imposed on the Commissioner's jurisdiction. And when asked to suggest ways in which the scheme might be improved 67.5 per cent of respondents replied, again as their first response, that the area open to the Commissioner's investigation should be extended, many of them specifically mentioning local government

29 See Roy Gregory and Alan Alexander, 'Our Parliamentary Ombudsman. Part II: Development and the Problem of Identity', *Public Administration*, Spring 1973.

30 *Ibid.*

Table 5

Perceived Effectiveness Levels of Parliamentary Techniques (percentages of MPs)

Perceived Effectiveness Levels	Parliamentary Techniques for Redress of Grievances					
	Parliamentary Question	Letter to Minister	Adjournment Debate	PCA	Approach Official	Talk to Minister
Highly Ineffective/ Ineffective	3.9	-	5.2	13.0	2.6	1.3
Somewhat Ineffective	18.2	1.3	11.7	16.9	5.2	2.6
Moderately Effective	35.1	20.8	36.4	19.5	22.1	18.2
Effective/ Highly Effective	23.4	71.4	29.9	22.1	36.4	61.1
Unclassified	19.4	6.5	16.8	28.5	33.7	16.8
Totals	100.0	100.0	100.0	100.0	100.0	100.0

SOURCE: Gregory and Alexander (1973)

as a field of administrative action which in their view ought to be brought within the Commissioner's jurisdiction.[31]

A good many changes have taken place, of course, since the 1970 survey was carried out, both in the Parliamentary Commissioner Scheme and in the United Kingdom Ombudsman arrangements generally. In 1973 provision was made for a Health Service Commissioner. Local Commissioners for Administration were appointed for England and Wales in 1974 and for Scotland in 1975. In 1987 a wide range of non-departmental public bodies were brought within the Commissioner's remit. The passing years, however, seem to have done little to raise the standing of the Parliamentary Commissioner scheme in the eyes of the MPs. Research conducted in 1989 indicated that only 19 per cent of MPs then surveyed found the Parliamentary Commissioner 'very useful'; whereas 67 per cent regarded the Office as 'only slightly useful' and 11 per cent considered it 'not at all useful'.[32]

By now, it seems, the main cause of MPs' dissatisfaction was the length of time taken by the Commissioner to complete his investigations and produce reports. The attention of the Select Committee had been drawn to this problem in 1986 when one MP complained to it about delay on the part of the Office in dealing with a case of alleged maladministration in the Ministry of Agriculture, Fisheries and Food. Though he had been an enthusiast of the appointment of a Parliamentary Commissioner this MP told the Select Committee, and still admired the quality of his investigations, he had had to advise his constituents that the Commissioner was 'so deplorably slow in his response' that he was 'not the effective channel of redress that Parliament intended when it passed the Parliamentary Commissioner Act'.[33]

The average 'throughput time' for investigations at this stage, the Commissioner revealed, had reached twelve months, which (he told the Select committee) he would have liked to reduce to nine or ten. Anything below that, he thought, would be 'unrealistic' and would risk 'sacrificing accuracy and thoroughness'.[34] A year later the Commissioner was able to report a slight reduction in the backlog of cases and to persuade the Select Committee that the continuing delay of a year or more in some investigations stemmed not from his Office but from departments.[35]

The extent of MPs' concern over the time taken to investigate complaints was confirmed in the 1989 survey referred to above. 'Delay' came highest on the list of 'problems' spontaneously noted by respondents, sixteen replies

31 *Ibid.*

32 See Gavin Drewry and Carol Harlow, loc.cit.

33 See *Second Report from the Select Committee, 1985-86*, H.C. 312, 25 March 1986, Minutes of Evidence, 23 July 1985, QQ.181-238.

34 *Ibid*, p.xiii.

35 See *Second Report from the Select Committee, 1986-87*, H.C. 251, 9 March 1987, p.v.

mentioning it, often as a reason for failure to use the Office. One respondent, it seems, described the handling of cases as 'very slow and long-winded'; a second noted that he tried to encourage constituents 'to take other action if possible' because of the length of time involved; and a third reflected MP's perception of a suitable turn-round time of six to nine weeks rather than the six to nine months which was commonplace in the Commissioner's Office.[36]

MPs' complaints about the Commissioner's jurisdiction and about delay on the part of the Office, however, may be only symptoms of a deeper problem, arising out of a less than perfect match between the needs and expectations of Members on the one hand and the role of the Parliamentary Commissioner, as it has developed in the United Kingdom, on the other. The work of the Parliamentary Ombudsman has been described by the Select Committee as 'an extension of that undertaken by MPs on a daily basis, albeit with different methods'.[37] Up to a point this is true. But as MPs have discovered, in some circumstance, far from operating as an extension of their own capabilities, the Parliamentary Ombudsman is a less effective grievance-man than themselves unaided.

With some justification, MPs have always regarded themselves as a species of 'constituency Ombudsman'. In this capacity, they go far and wide, if not particularly deep. Strictly speaking, the remit of MPs runs only to administrative action taken by central government departments for which Ministers are accountable to Parliament; in practice, of course, they receive and take up complaints against all manner of public authorities. They also take up all manner of complaints. Their 'Ombudsman efforts' are certainly not confined to cases of alleged maladministration. What is more, whilst MPs often fail to secure a favourable outcome to their enquires, they can usually be sure of getting a result, one way or the other, within a reasonably short period of time.

On the other hand, MPs are also in some respects 'fettered Ombudsmen'. No doubt they sometimes secure 'mediatory' solutions to constituents' problems and very occasionally persuade Ministers to cancel, vary and reverse discretionary decisions taken without any suggestion of maladministration. But MPs do not have access to civil servants and departmental files. Nor does any particular authority attach to their opinions if and when they find themselves at odds with Ministers and officials, not about matters of fact, but about what constitutes good and bad administration.

It was, of course, the ability of the Office to fill gaps in their own armoury which Government spokesmen had been at pains to emphasise when the Parliamentary Commissioner scheme was introduced in the mid 1960s. As we have seen, the Office was indeed described as 'a new and powerful weapon', designed to enable MPs to do a better job on behalf of their

36 See Gavin Drewry and Carol Harlow, loc.cit.

37 See *First Report from the Select Committee, 1990-91,* p.xii.

constituents. It was soon brought home to MPs, however, that over large areas of their own work this 'new servant of the House' could offer them no assistance at all. Furthermore, as the Parliamentary Commissioner scheme evolved, it also became increasingly apparent that, even when the Commissioner was authorised to investigate their constituents' complaints, for MPs' purposes the utility of the office was very much thrown into question by another, highly distinctive, feature of the United Kingdom's variant of the Ombudsman institution.

There are significant differences, of course, between the role of an Ombudsman and the 'Ombudsman role' as performed by MPs. Elected representatives are *ex parte* advocates; they see themselves as 'people's champions'. This is not the approach adopted by most Ombudsmen. As Ombudsmen see it, they are obliged to adopt a position of neutrality and impartiality between complainants and authorities subject to complaint:

> 'An Ombudsman is not the citizen's lawyer or advocate. He has a duty of objectivity which would be incompatible with such an approach ... He is not the citizen's lawyer for the simple reason that if his investigation vindicates the actions of the civil servant he must not hesitate to uphold him.'[38]

Clearly, this is very much the view taken by the present Parliamentary Commissioner. As he told the Select Committee in December 1991, his reports were not always 'comfortable to the Government'; but because he was 'wholly dispassionate' neither were they always entirely comfortable to those who made the complaints in the first place.[39]

In the United Kingdom, moreover, the divergence between the role of the Parliamentary Commissioner and the Ombudsman role as played by MPs had been further accentuated by the emphasis which successive Commissioners have placed upon the 'audit function' of the Office. All Ombudsman institutions have a range of essential characteristics in common. At the same time, the office of Ombudsman is also very much what incumbents choose to make it. Some see their primary task as that of securing redress for individual complainants. Others, whilst concerned to remedy individual cases of injustice, take the view that their most important function is to monitor the general fairness and efficiency of the administrative apparatus subject to their scrutiny.[40]

---

38 See Arthur Maloney, 'The Ombudsman as mediator, Reformer and Fighter?', in Gerald E Caiden, op.cit., p.71; see also Larry B Hill, 'The Self-Perceptions of Ombudsmen: A Comparative Survey', *ibid*, pp.50-2.

39 See *Second Report from the Select Committee, 1991-91,* Q.66. As the Commissioner also points out, the fact that he is 'independent' enables him to give departments a 'clean bill of health' (in a way the Ministers cannot) when he finds that complaints are not justified.

40 See B Serota, 'The Evolution of the Role of the Ombudsman - Comparisons and Perspectives', in Gerald E Caiden (ed), op.cit., p.29.

Philosophical differences of this kind may, in turn, lead to different methods of working, just as can differing procedural requirements prescribed by the originating legislation. As a former Local Government Ombudsman points out:

'... if the primary objective is to procure satisfactory action for individuals, this may be achieved without any real investigation of the administrative act that led to the complaint. A telephone call to a particular official might produce a solution without the need to establish whether the official's previous action should be criticised. But if the Ombudsman's primary objective is to investigate the administrative actions of the official, then the quick settlement approach will not be enough.'[41]

Much the same point is made by an Australian State Ombudsman. Many of his cases, he observes, are settled without the need for 'any strident process of formal criticism'. The success and achievements of the Ombudsman, he agrees, are often measured by the percentage of cases cleared up in this 'quite' manner. But as he also goes on to point out;

'There is, of course, another value in the Ombudsman process, the added role of promoting and facilitating an extended form of public accountability of agencies for their administrative actions. Such a role cannot generally be realised in the quiet streams of settlement and 'quick fix' operations which may be favoured by the individual complainant. It will come to the fore only with a formal and thorough, thus necessarily more lengthy process of investigation involving inspection of relevant documents, reports and examination of witnesses.'[42]

What is more, if an Ombudsman does see his role as that of performing an 'administrative audit', involving an appraisal of the conduct of officials subject to complaint, the question of fairness inevitably arises. As one observer with a legal background puts it:

'A report which characterises a bureaucratic action as 'unreasonable, unjust, oppressive or improperly discriminatory', to use the words of the South Australian statute, may do irreparable harm to the bureaucrat concerning whom the report is made. If the report is ill-conceived and unjustified it may be difficult if not impossible to rectify the harm which results.'[43]

An audit implies the possibility of criticism, and clearly criticism can be justified only if the Ombudsman's findings are based upon complete and thorough investigations.

---

41 *Ibid.*

42 See Eugene Biganovsky "'Policy - Administration' - Jurisdiction of Ombudsman', Paper presented to the Twelfth Conference of Australasian and Pacific Ombudsmen, Adelaide, 7-11 October 1991.

43 See Roma Mitchell, Governor of South Australia, Address to Twelfth Conference of Australasian and Pacific Ombudsmen.

If some Ombudsmen make the provision of 'quick fix solutions' their main priority, and others concentrate upon promoting an 'extended form of public accountability', there is not much doubt as to the category into which the Parliamentary Commissioner falls. In the United Kingdom, it is suggested, the time and care taken to investigate complaints is greater than in any other country served by an Ombudsman system.[44]

The Office of Parliamentary Commissioner was to some extent modelled on that of the Comptroller and Auditor General; and the first Commissioner, Sir Edmund Compton, was himself a former Comptroller and Audit General, used to 'ferreting out' by very careful investigations the possible misuse of public funds. In his new role as Parliamentary Commissioner, it is suggested, Sir Edmund saw his major task as that of similarly uncovering official maladministration of other kinds. As he told the Select Committee in 1970:

> 'My function is to investigate the action taken by a department and decide whether there has been maladministration by the department. So my primary job as investigator - and I am sure this must be right - is to ascertain by inquiry inside the department what those departmental actions were.'[45]

It was very important, Sir Edmund maintained, 'to go in depth into those parts of the case which seemed to merit investigation'. In his view it was an 'absolute principle of investigations' that his enquiries should be carried out first-hand. He did not feel that he could rely on reports from departments on their own investigations of complaints.[46]

It is, of course, true that the investigative procedures followed by the office are in part determined by statute. Section 7(1) of the Parliamentary Commissioner Act requires the Commissioner to begin an investigation by allowing the Principal Officer of the department concerned to comment on the allegations contained in the complaint. Thus in 'stage 1' of the process, as Sir Edmund described it, there is in effect an investigation by the government department complained against similar to - but not identical with - that which would have taken place had a Member of Parliament taken up a constituent's complaint directly with the Minister rather than with the Commissioner. These internal inquiries provide the Office with a full statement of the facts known to the department, and of its view of the case, often with supporting evidence.

Nothing in the legislation, however, requires the Commissioner to go beyond obtaining a statement about a complaint from the department being investigated. But whereas in New Zealand (for example) about three-quarters

44 See W B Gwyn, 'The Conduct of Ombudsman Investigations of Complaints' in G E Caiden (ed), op.cit., p.88. For the Commissioner's investigation process, see R Gregory and P Hutchesson, op.cit., pp.148-72.

45 See W B Gwyn (1982), p.87.

46 *Ibid.*

of the Ombudsman's investigations and conclusions rely solely on evidence of this kind, in the United Kingdom only about 5-10 per cent of the Parliamentary Commissioner's investigations, it seems, are limited to an examination by the Commissioner of the department's report on the complaint.

The overwhelming majority of the Commissioner's cases move on to 'stage 2'. In something like 90-95 per cent of inquiries the Commissioner's investigators see the relevant files, which are for the most part sent to the Office for examination. In about 40-45 per cent of cases the officials concerned are questioned, in their departments, by the Commissioner's staff. And in about 60 per cent of cases the complainants themselves are interviewed in their homes, partly because aggrieved persons find such visits satisfying, and partly because complainants are sometimes in a position to supply information unknown to the department.[47]

The final stage in the Commissioner's investigation occurs after he has accepted draft reports on the results of his inquiries. Before the report is forwarded to the MP referring the complaint the Commissioner sends it to the agency concerned for comment on the accuracy of its factual content. This practice has been adopted partly to give Ministers an opportunity to exercise their authority under Section 11(3) of the Parliamentary Commissioner Act to prevent information appearing in the report which they believe to be prejudicial to the public interest; and partly to act as a final check on the accuracy of the reported facts of the case which rules out any possibility of departments, when they are criticised, subsequently arguing that the Commissioner had his facts wrong.[48]

Given an investigative procedure of this kind it is not perhaps surprising that the Commissioner takes so long over his cases. In part, the *modus operandi* adopted by the Office is dictated by the 1967 Act. But what mainly accounts for the distinctive character assumed by the United Kingdom Ombudsman, the argument runs, is the 'role perception' of the first Commissioner, which over time has become institutionalised.[49]

However that may be, confirmation of the enduring influence exercised by the original incumbent of the Office is provided by the present Parliamentary Commissioner, William Reid. Recalling that the first Commissioner was Sir Edmund Compton, a former Comptroller and Auditor General, he notes that 'the foundations which he laid so effectively have stood the test of time', and

---

47 *Ibid.* For complainants visited in their own homes by the Commissioner's investigators the United Kingdom Ombudsmen arrangements, it is pointed out, provide a personal touch absent in (for example) New Zealand and Scandinavia.

48 *Ibid.*

49 *Ibid*, p.88; for further comment on the distinctive 'audit role' of the United Kingdom Parliamentary Commissioner, see Frank Stacey, *Ombudsmen Compared* (Clarendon Press), pp.135-7.

points out that the investigation procedure initiated by Sir Edmund in 1967 is 'still in its essentials the one used'.[50]

Significantly, the present Commissioner also confirms that whilst his 'primary task' is to investigate 'a complaint about action or inaction said to have led to injustice for an individual', he regards 'his activities also to be an external control audit of the organisations complained about'. And drawing attention to the importance he attaches to the 'audit' aspect of his work, with its emphasis on the improvement of administrative practices, he continues:

> 'If I can produce redress for a wronged individual, that is a good thing. It is even better if I can suggest or encourage a change of procedures or systems by the organisation complained against, which will diminish the chance of the circumstances which led to the complaint recurring. I emphasise the need for public administrators ... to improve their communication skills, to listen to the public, to minimise delay, to give reasons for their actions, and to concede that appeals and decisions on complaints are openly fairer when decided by an agency external to the one against which the complaint lies.'[51]

This is a perspective very different from that of MPs. Members no doubt regard an 'external quality control audit' as a good thing in its way, just as they value the work of the Comptroller and Auditor General. On occasions they also doubtless recognise that it is the very de luxe quality of the Commissioner's investigations which does the trick, and helps secure remedial action previously denied their constituents.[52] But for the most part when MPs take up complainants' cases they are not concerned to discover in detail exactly what officials did and why. Only secondarily are they interested in whether or not administrators have behaved properly. Their main interest is certainly not in the improvement of administrative procedures and systems for the future. What chiefly concerns MPs is the outcome of their cases, and how matters stand at the end of the day.

Given the Parliamentary Commissioner's philosophy and the requirements of the 1967 Act on the one hand, and the very different preoccupations of MPs on the other, the chances of enhancing the value of the Office in the eyes of MPs, and therefore of increasing the use they make of it, are clearly limited. This is not to say, however, that nothing can be done more effectively to realise the full potential of the Office.

---

50 See William Reid, 'An Independent Voice', *The House Magazine*, 20 January 1992.

51 *Ibid.*

52 See, for example, Roy Gregory and Gavin Drewry, 'Barlow Clowes and the Ombudsman', Part II, *Public Law*, Autumn 1991.

III

In the twenty-five years of its existence the Office of Parliamentary Commissioner has clearly established itself as a valuable addition to the apparatus of complaint-handling mechanisms available to United Kingdom citizens. Few institutions, however, work so well that they cannot be improved. So far as the Parliamentary Commissioner scheme is concerned there is reason to think that the Office could with advantage be more extensively used. But the problem is not simply one of increasing the Commissioner's case-load. There would be no point in bringing into the Office for investigation complaints which could equally well be cleared up by other means. Nor should it be forgotten that, in terms of grievances redressed and avoided, changes in administrative practice and procedures effected by the Commissioner in the performance of his 'audit function' are no less valuable than the provision of remedies in individual cases. It might be difficult, some would argue, to retain the 'quality control' side of the Commissioner's work if a larger case-load meant that complaints could no longer be investigated with the care and thoroughness which has always marked virtually all inquiries undertaken by the Office. That said, there do appear to be some things which most observers agree need to be done if the Parliamentary Commissioner scheme is to be employed more widely and to better effect.

If, as seems likely, MPs rely very largely on constituents to take the initiative in asking for complaints to be referred, clearly the extent of public awareness of the Office and its functions must be increased if more cases are to find their way to the Parliamentary Commissioner for investigation. Over the years, Commissioners have adopted a variety of methods - press, radio and television interviews, accepting invitations to address universities, schools, clubs, societies and local 'multipliers' such as Citizens Advice Bureaux, and the distribution of posters and information leaflets - in an effort to make the existence and activities of the Office better known to potential complainants.[53] Clearly it is essential that activities of this kind should continue. But as the Parliamentary Commissioner pointed out in 1977, 'the most effective form of publicity is probably the publication of reports of specific investigations'.[54] Agreeing that this was so, in 1978 the Select Committee invited the Commissioner to consider selection a greater number of cases each year for the purpose of occasional reports under Section 10(4) of the Act, instead of including them in his regular publications of the edited texts of the reports he had made to Members.[55] For

53 See, for example, Parliamentary Commissioner, *Annual Report for 1977*, H.C. 157, 26 January 1978, paras. 5-10; *Annual Report for 1979*, H.C. 402, (n.d), para. 12; *Annual Report for 1982*, H.C. 257, 23 March 1983, para. 13.

54 See Parliamentary Commissioner, *Annual Report for 1977*, para. 8.

55 See *Fourth Report from the Select Committee, 1979-78*, p.xi.

reasons that are not clear, few such reports have in fact been published. More of them would certainly serve to keep the Commissioner in the public eye.

Nor is there any reason why governmental bodies subject to investigation by the Commissioner should not help publicise the work of the Office. In evidence to the Select Committee the Commissioner points out that the Citizen's Charter, published as a White Paper in July 1991, makes reference to complaints procedures and the need for independent complaints machinery. He notes that whilst in the section on the National Health Service the White Paper helpfully notes that complaints may be made to the independent Health Service Commissioner, no equivalent mention is made of the Parliamentary Commissioner in the passage about prisons which follows, although such complaints may be referred via a Member to the Office.[56] As the Commissioner goes on to point out, throughout the White Paper there is reference to forthcoming charters dealing with particular services, among those envisaged being charters for patients, parents, tax-payers, passengers, families, job seekers, national insurance contributors, those deriving benefits from the Social Security Benefits Agency and others. While the best way of settling complaints, the Commissioner acknowledges, is to provide means for a quick local solution, where that does not resolve disputes it is essential that the complainant should be informed by the organisation he is dealing with how to take matters further. In that connection, the Commissioner goes on:

> 'It would be very helpful if the practice adopted by the Tax-payers' Charter were widely followed. That Charter indicates clearly how to appeal to external tribunals or to the Parliamentary Commissioner when complaints are not settled. References to customer service managers and to clear procedures for handling enquiries and difficulties locally are welcome but internal complaints procedures alone do not provide either the *independent* investigation of complaints which characterises the Parliamentary Commissioner's activities, or the access to independent tribunals which is so important for the rights of a citizen.'[57]

In subsequent evidence given to the Select Committee on behalf of the Government it was indicated that the charter programme provided an opportunity to ensure that people are aware of the role of the Parliamentary Commissioner. For its part, the Select Committee has expressed some concern that the sheer variety of complaints procedures which may be available should not divert attention away from the Commissioner's role. Central guidance from the Government, the Committee maintains, should emphasise to staff the importance of directing potentially dissatisfied complainants, whose grievances

56 See *Second Report from the Select Committee, 1991-92,* pp.12-13.
57 *Ibid.*

might not have been remedied by internal review, towards the Parliamentary Commissioner. In particular, the Committee observed, leaflets on how to complain about Government services should mention the Commissioner's role, as does the Jobseeker's Charter published in December 1991.[58]

Given the key role played in the Parliamentary Commissioner scheme by MPs, it is of course equally important that they should be aware of the Office and its functions. As the Select Committee observed in 1978, it considered that there was a need for the Commissioner's work to be brought more forcefully to the attention not only of the general public but also of MPs.[59] Quite possibly more could be done to this effect. Commenting on the Parliamentary Commissioner's Annual Report for 1989 the Select Committee notes that it includes one paragraph about the publicity efforts of the Office, but 'curiously' makes no mention of MPs who must refer cases. The Select Committee went on to suggest to the Commissioner that when the leaflet about his role was revised a copy should be sent to all MPs with a covering letter.[60] This suggestion was duly acted upon by the Commissioner.[61]

Though the Government has shown no great enthusiasm for the idea, the Select Committee has also long been of the opinion that one of the most effective ways of 'raising consciousness' among MPs about the role and work of the Office is by debate on the floor of the House of Commons. The very announcement of such debates, the Committee argues, would alert MPs to the Commissioner's existence, even if they did not attend them. The debates themselves, the Committee argues, would also provide a sharper focus for media interest.[62]

In its Report published in December 1990 the Select Committee looked forward 'to further efforts by the Parliamentary Commissioner to enhance knowledge of his work and role among MPs'.[63] Exactly what the Commissioner was expected to do was left unclear. There is, however, one simple but important point which seems to be overlooked or disregarded by many MPs. As the Chairman of the Select Committee put it:

---

58 *Ibid*, p.viii. This is a significant development because, of course, few organisations, public or private, are keen to advertise the complaint-handling mechanisms to which aggrieved citizens or customers may resort. Commenting on the 'strong reluctance' often found among administrators to say to aggrieved persons 'if you do not accept my decision you can go to the Ombudsman', a former United Kingdom Local Ombudsman notes that the public library close to the Local Ombudsman's London office displays posters telling citizens how to complain about a wide range of agencies, but not about the local authority that runs the library; see B Serota, 'The Evolution of the Role of the Ombudsman - Comparisons and Perspectives', in Gerald E Caiden (ed), op.cit., p.36.

59 See *Fourth Report from the Select Committee, 1977-78*, p.x.

60 See *First Report from the Select Committee, 1990-91*, p.xii.

61 See *Fourth Report from the Select Committee, 1990-91*, p.vi.

62 See *First Report from the Select Committee, 1990-91*, p.xiii.

63 *Ibid.*

'The Parliamentary Ombudsman system can only work if MPs continue to be willing to refer cases to him *and recommend the referral to constituents unaware of the Ombudsman's existence.*'[64]

This something which ought surely to be brought to Members' notice with more force than hitherto.

But if under-utilisation is related chiefly to the lukewarm attitude of MPs towards the Office and its operations, no amount of additional publicity for the Parliamentary Commissioner scheme will persuade Members to make more use of it. A short way with this problem would of course be not to remove the causes of MPs' discontent but rather to remove MPs from the referral procedure. If there were direct access of the Office it would matter not what members felt about Parliamentary Commissioner scheme, for then they would no longer be in a position to determine the number of cases reaching the Office for investigation.

There seems little chance, however, of such a change being made. In the 'Review of Access and Jurisdiction' it published in July 1978 the Select Committee concluded that there was no need for direct access to the Parliamentary Commissioner, approving instead the 'revised system of indirect access' introduced by the Commissioner as from the Spring of 1978.[65] Subsequently, in its Report published in December 1990 the Select Committee declared that, in its view, the distinctive role of MPs in the British system justified the continuance of the MP filter, whereby cases had to be referred by a Member before consideration by the Commissioner.[66] In written evidence submitted to the Select Committee in November 1991 the present Parliamentary Commissioner, William Reid, commented that 'on the basis of comparison with most foreign jurisdictions and with the Local Government Ombudsmen in England, Scotland and Wales, it may be potentially disadvantageous to some complainants that they have to approach the PCA through a Member of the House of Commons'.[67] The Select Committee, however, reported that it continued to believe that the advantages of the current system outweighed its disadvantages.[68] As for the generality of Members, it is noteworthy that the one aspect of the Parliamentary

64 Author's emphasis added. See Sir Antony Buck, 'Providing a Link', *The House Magazine*, 20 January 1992.

65 Under this revised procedure the Commissioner undertook to offer to send *prima facie* investigable complaints received direct from members of the public, together with any accompanying papers, to the constituent's MP, saying that he was prepared to start an investigation should the MP wish him to do so; see *Fourth Report from the Select Committee, 1977-78,* p.ix.

66 See *First Report from the Select Committee, 1990-91,* p.xii.

67 See *Second Report from the Select Committee, 1991-92,* p.12.

68 *Ibid,* p.viii.

Commissioner scheme endorsed by substantial majorities in both the 1970 and 1989 surveys was the provision for indirect access via MPs.[69]

If a change to direct access is not yet in the realms of practical politics, it may none the less be possible to alleviate the problem of under-utilisation by doing something to lessen the dissatisfaction evidently felt by many MPs with the way in which the Parliamentary Commissioner currently operates. As we saw in Part II, what mainly concerns MPs are the restrictions placed on the area open to investigation by the Commissioner; and the length of time taken by the Office to complete its inquiries and issue reports.

So far as the Commissioner's jurisdiction is concerned, as the Select Committee notes, this has been one of its 'abiding concerns' ever since the Office was established in 1967.[70] As Table 2 indicates, in every year in the history of the Parliamentary Commissioner scheme more than 50 per cent of the cases referred by MPs have been rejected by the Commissioner as being outwith his jurisdiction. In the 1980s the percentages were even higher than in the 1970s and 1960s.

It is true that from time to time extensions have been made to the area open to investigation by the Commissioner. In 1979, for example, the actions of career consular officials abroad in relation to UK citizens with the right of abode in the United Kingdom were brought under the Commissioner's jurisdiction.[71] Subsequently, by means of the Parliamentary Commissioner (Consular Complaints) Act 1981, the Commissioner's jurisdiction was further extended so as to enable British citizens resident overseas to make complaints about the quality of the assistance they receive from consular officials. Something like a hundred non-departmental bodies were brought within the Commissioner's remit by the Parliamentary and Health Service Commissioner Act 1987. And a long dispute between the Commissioner and Select Committee on the one hand, and the Lord Chancellor's Department on the other was brought to an end by the inclusion within the Court and Legal Services Act 1990 of provisions permitting 'administrative functions exercisable by any person appointed by the Lord Chancellor as a member of the administrative staff of any court or tribunal' to be investigated by the Commissioner, though excluding action 'taken at the direction, or on the authority (whether express or implied), of any person acting in a judicial capacity or in his capacity as member of the tribunal'.[72]

69 In the 1970 survey, 75 per cent of MPs were 'opposed' or 'strongly opposed' to direct access; only 13 per cent expressed support for a change in the scheme to permit aggrieved persons to approach the Commissioner direct; see Roy Gregory and Alan Alexander, loc.cit. Nearly two decades later, in the 1989 survey, 23 per cent of MPs questioned were in favour of direct access, 67 per cent were opposed, and 8.5 per cent offered no response; see Gavin Drewry and Carol Harlow, loc.cit.

70 See *First Report from the Select Committee, 1990-91*, p.v.

71 See S.I. 1979 No. 915.

72 See *First Report from the Select Committee, 1990-91*, pp.iv-vii.

But as the Select Committee points out, little progress has been made in extending the Commissioner's jurisdiction to other important areas of central government excluded from his remit by Schedule 3 to the Parliamentary Commissioner Act 1967. These include 'action taken in matters relating to contractual and commercial transactions' and 'action taken in respect of appointments or removals, pay, discipline, superannuation or other personnel matters' in relation to Crown servants subject to investigation. The exclusion from the Commissioner's jurisdiction of Crown personnel matters has been a particular bone of contention between the Select Committee and successive Governments over many years. And as the Committee has made clear, it remains of the opinion that complaints arising prior to appointment to the civil service and after retirement should be within the Commissioner's remit. As it also points out, this may be a matter of increasing importance as the trend towards devolved recruitment in the civil service gathers pace.[73]

The fact is of course that the exclusion from the Commissioner's jurisdiction of none of the 'matters not subject to investigation' listed in Schedule 3 to the 1967 Act has ever been justified in terms of the original rationale of the Parliamentary Commissioner scheme, for as its architects explained at the outset the function of the office was to strengthen the machinery of Parliamentary surveillance over administrative action by providing MPs with a new instrument for investigating 'the area of Ministerial and therefore of Parliamentary control'. Clearly, there was therefore no case in principle for excluding from the Commissioner's remit anything it was open to MPs to take up with Ministers.

Approaching the same issue from a different angle, in its Report published in December 1990 the Select Committee points out that in both Sweden and Denmark there appears to be a presumption in favour of decisions of public servants being subject to investigation by the Ombudsman, unless there is a sound reason to the contrary. The Committee goes on to declare:

> 'We believe that a similar presumption could and should operate in the United Kingdom, namely, that all decisions of civil servants and others within appropriate departments and public bodies involving maladministration should be subject to investigation by the Parliamentary Commissioner for Administration, unless any constitutional principle, such as the independence of the judiciary dictates otherwise.'[74]

That surely is the guiding rule which ought to determine what is and is not made subject to investigation by the Commissioner. It is a principle which, if adopted by the Government, would serve to widen the Commissioner's jurisdiction, increase the number of cases referred to and investigated by the

73 *Ibid*, p.vi.
74 *Ibid*.

Office, and at the same time do much to remove the restricted nature of the Commissioner's remit as a cause of dissatisfaction reducing the value of the Office in the estimation of MPs.

Considerations of this kind relate to what might be termed the 'spatial' aspects of the Commissioner's jurisdiction. Rather different issues are raised by another restriction on his remit, namely the provision authorising the Office to investigate only cases in which aggrieved persons claim to have suffered 'injustice in consequence of maladministration'.

In its critique of the Parliamentary Commissioner scheme published in 1977 JUSTICE proposed that the Commissioner 'should no longer be limited to investigating complaints about 'maladministration', and argued that instead he should be empowered to 'investigate and report on' acts and omissions which were 'unreasonable, unjust or oppressive'.[75] But as the Commissioner pointed out, the term 'maladministration' had been interpreted with great flexibility by himself and his predecessors. As he also made clear, there was nothing anyway in the 1967 Act to prevent him from investigating complaints to the effect that the actions of government departments had been 'unjust or oppressive'. An 'unreasonable' act, he acknowledged, was difficult to define. He believed, however, that in practice he would have no difficulty in investigating a complaint of this kind.[76]

What sometimes complicates discussion is the fact that the term 'maladministration' is used not only in relation to the Commissioner's jurisdiction but also to delimit his 'competence', that is, the grounds on which he is authorised to criticise or question administrative action subject to complaint. Section 10(3) of the 1967 Act provides that, if after conducting an investigation, it appears to the Commissioner that injustice has been caused to the person aggrieved in consequence of maladministration, and that injustice has not been, or will not be remedied, he may, if he thinks fit, lay before each House of Parliament a special report on the case. And s.12(3) declares that nothing in the Act authorises or requires the Commissioner to question the merits of a decision taken without maladministration by a government department or other authority in the exercise of a discretion vested in that department or authority.

Given what the Commissioner has said about his interpretation of 'maladministration' in connection with jurisdiction; and bearing in mind that since 1968 the Commissioner has operated on the principle, recommended by the Select Committee, that 'if he finds a decision which ... appears to him to be thoroughly bad in quality, he might infer from the quality of the decision itself that there had been an element of maladministration in the taking of it',

75 See JUSTICE, op.cit., p.25.

76 See *Second Report of the Parliamentary Commissioner*, 1977-78, H.C. 157, 26 January 1978, para. 19.

there would appear to be little scope in practice for further enlarging the grounds on which administrative action could legitimately be open to criticism by the Commissioner. This was the view taken by the Select Committee in its Report published in July 1978 when it concluded that no change was needed in the definition of maladministration.

Furthermore, to judge from the Commissioner's Annual Reports, confining his competence to 'maladministration' seems not to have restricted unduly his scope for characterising as defective or faulty in some way the administrative action he investigates. As Table 1 indicates, throughout the 1970s and 1980s he regularly found 30 or 40 per cent of the complaints he investigated wholly justified; in many other cases he found it necessary (while not upholding the main complaint) to criticise at least some aspects of departments' handling of matters.[77]

If there is indeed no case for extending the concept of 'maladministration' in relation to the Commissioner's competence, nothing would be gained by redefining the term in connection with his jurisdictional remit. Clearly, there would be no point in permitting the Commissioner to admit for investigation (say) cases in which complainants took exception, essentially, to the 'merits' of discretionary decisions, if at the end of the inquiry it was beyond the Commissioner's competence to question the merits *per se* of such decisions taken without maladministration.

The other main cause of MPs' dissatisfaction with the Parliamentary Commissioner scheme relates to the 'throughput time' taken by the Commissioner to report on complaints investigated. In 1989 the diversion of time and effort required to deal with the Barlow Clowes affair not surprisingly had the effect of putting a brake on the Office's drive to increase the output of reports and to bring down the time taken over individual cases. The average throughput time, consequently, rose from just over twelve months in 1988 to slightly over fifteen months in 1989. This increase, the Select Committee noted, was regrettable, particularly since, as the Commissioner himself had recognised, even twelve months was much longer than the referring Member and indeed the aggrieved citizen should have to wait.[78]

As the Select Committee acknowledged, the speed with which investigations are completed depends in part on the response time of the departments concerned. All departments, the Select Committee emphasised, were expected to respond to the Commissioner's initial inquiry within six weeks. In 1989, the Committee was told, there had been only seven cases in which a response was not received within this maximum period. The efforts

77 In 1989, for example, the Commissioner upheld 48 per cent of complaints investigated; in almost as many cases again (42 per cent) he was critical of departmental action while not finding that the faulty administration in question had inflicted injustice on the complainants; see *First Report from the Select Committee, 1990-91,* p.xii.

78 See *First Report from the Select Committee, 1990-91,* p.iv.

made by departments in this regard, the Select Committee observed, called for a matching change in the speed of work in the Office itself. Agreeing that this was so, the Commissioner outlined various measures he had taken to accelerate the production of reports 'with no loss of thoroughness' in the investigations. The increase in throughput time, the Commissioner told the Select Committee, had been checked, and as the backlog of old cases was eliminated, he said, it ought to be possible to make progress towards 'the ambitious target' of nine months as the average time for the investigation of cases.[79]

There were signs in the course of the following year, it was reported, that the Commissioner's efforts were beginning to pay off. By the end of 1990, the Commissioner told the Select Committee in April 1991, as a result of 'hard pounding' on his part the average length of time taken to complete investigations had fallen to thirteen months and ten days, a 20 per cent reduction from the beginning of the year. Assuring the Committee that he would 'keep on pounding', the Commissioner said that he had set as 'an interim target' an average throughput time of twelve months.[80]

Given the *de luxe* quality of the Commissioner's investigations, an average throughput time of nine months may indeed represent an ambitious long-term target. But even nine months is a period of a quite different order from the time taken by other grievance-handling mechanisms available to MPs. So that even if the Commissioner succeeds in achieving his target, doing so may not be enough by itself significantly to change MPs' perceptions of the usefulness of the Office for their purposes. They were concerned about the problem of 'despatch' after all, in the days when the Commissioner's throughput time was a good deal shorter than nine months. So far as 'throughput time is concerned, though it might go against the grain, arguably the only way of persuading Members to take a markedly more favourable view of the Parliamentary Commissioner scheme might be for the Office to accept some 'loss of thoroughness' in order to reduce substantially the time taken over at least some of the complaints investigated.

It is interesting in this connection to recall the view put forward in 1977 by JUSTICE, which argued that the 'very thorough' method of investigation followed by the Commissioner was 'unnecessary for the more routine or simple type of case', in which 'a telephoned inquiry could often produce a change in decision and immediate redress to the complainant'. The Commissioner, JUSTICE suggested, should adopt simpler methods for dealing with many complaints alongside his very thorough, 'Rolls Royce', method of investigation which would still have its place for the more difficult cases.[81]

79 *Ibid.*

80 See *Fourth Report from the Select Committee, 1990-91*, p.v.

81 See JUSTICE, op.cit., pp.6-7.

A procedure which appears to operate along these lines has in fact been introduced in Northern Ireland. In his Annual Report for 1990 the Northern Ireland Parliamentary Commissioner explains that the Screening Section of his Office attempts to resolve complaints falling within his jurisdiction on an informal basis if it is clear that 'there is no evidence of serious maladministration and it is likely that the matter can be resolved speedily without recourse to formal investigation and report'. In general, he observes, it appears that complainants are happy to see matters dealt with in this way, particularly if it means that their complaint is redressed within the shortest possible time.

The adoption of a 'two-tier system of investigation', the Northern Ireland Commissioner maintains, does not reflect any lack of concern to deal with maladministration where it exists. He continues:

> 'If the complaint arises from a single lapse, or a minor deviation from the rules, I will generally be satisfied if the complainant is given his or her due and an apology in appropriate terms. If the administrative failings while still relatively minor, reflect a systemic weakness or a lack of clarity in the instructions I will generally write to the Permanent Secretary or Chief Officer calling his attention to the case and suggesting that he might wish to review the procedures. If my preliminary enquiries, which can be quite searching, and involve my officers inspecting files and speaking to officials, disclose either the possibility of serious maladministration or a pattern of persistent failure to observe reasonable standards, then I will give formal notice and begin a formal investigation.'

In 1990, the Commissioner reported, 81 cases had been cleared without formal investigation, and 26 cases were accepted for formal investigation. The average time taken between receiving a complaint, investigating and issuing a report, he noted, had been thirteen months. Informal enquiries, on the other hand, had been generally dealt with by telephone or fax, and had produced, usually, an immediate reply. The average time for disposing of a complaint informally had been six weeks, and some had been dealt with in as little as one or two weeks.[82]

Whether a 'two-tier' approach of this kind, which has been welcomed by the Select Committee,[83] would be compatible with the requirements of the 1967 Act is not altogether clear. But it is certainly a possibility worth consideration, both as a means of ensuring that some cases at least are dealt with more speedily, thereby raising the esteem of the Office in the eyes of

82 See *Annual Report of the Northern Ireland Parliamentary Commissioner for Administration and Commissioner for Complaints for 1990*, H.C. 182, 31 January 1991, pp.4, 5 and 8.

83 See *Second Report from the Select Committee, 1990-91*, H.C. 167, 6 March 1991, p.v.

MPs, and also as a solution to the problem of dealing with more cases if greater public awareness and enhanced 'MP satisfaction' should result in a substantial increase in the number of referrals.

A 'fast-track' procedure of the kind operated by the Northern Ireland Parliamentary Commissioner is not necessarily the only method of dealing more quickly with some of the complaints referred to the Office. As we saw in Part II, having obtained a statement of the facts known to the department concerned, in virtually every case admitted for investigation the Parliamentary Commissioner proceeds to 'stage 2' and conducts his own full-scale inquiry. But, it is suggested, there is no reason why the Commissioner should not, like other Ombudsmen, vary the degree of thoroughness with which he investigates to accord with the complexity and significance of the complaints presented to him. In some cases, it is argued, the facts are not in dispute; what is at issue between complainants and the agencies complained against is the construction or interpretation which should be placed upon the facts. In these circumstances, it is suggested, the department's version of the story will provide the Commissioner with all he requires by way of factual information. The function of the Parliamentary Commissioner in cases of this kind, it is argued, should be not to duplicate the internal investigations carried out by a department, but to evaluate the department's performance in the light of his own standards of what constitutes good and bad administration.[84]

Any procedure which omitted 'stage 2' of the Commissioner's current inquiry process would of course be open to objections. For a start, it is of course true that when an Ombudsman relies upon agencies subject to complaint to provide the facts it is always possible that discreditable or unacceptable administrative conduct, which would have been uncovered by an external investigation, will remain concealed. The first Parliamentary Commissioner once told the Select Committee that if he had made a practice of accepting admissions of error as a reason for not enquiring further, departments might have been tempted to acknowledge one mistake or relatively unimportant shortcomings in the hope of avoiding a more thorough investigation leading to the disclosure of additional or worse defects.[85] On the other hand, since departments are aware that the Commissioner may in any case carry out his own investigation if he thinks fit, that consideration alone would in all probability act as a strong deterrent if they ever felt inclined to tell the Office less than the full story.

It could also be argued that if the Parliamentary Commissioner does not bring to the investigation of every case something that goes well beyond what MPs can do on their own by setting in train an internal investigation

84 See W B Gwyn, 'The Conduct of Ombudsman Investigations of Complaints', in G E Caiden (ed), op.cit., pp.88-9.

85 See *First Report from the Select Committee, 1970-71*, Minutes of Evidence, 25 March 1970, Q.106.

(that is to say, unless the Office does operate a 'stage 2' inquiry) there is little point in having the institution at all.

To this objection to the introduction of a 'two-tier' procedure there are two answers. In the first place, even when the Office had not carried out its own investigation the Commissioner would still be in a position to provide an authoritative external evaluation (which has no counterpart in the procedure initiated by MPs) of the administrative action subject to scrutiny. And secondly, the internal procedures set in motion within departments in response to a request for comments from the Commissioner are by no means identical with those activated by inquiries from MPs. Complaints forwarded by MPs to Ministers are of course investigated with care and attention. The internal investigations undertaken by departments following inquiries from MPs are, however, geared to replies which will be 'painted with a broad brush'. The Commissioner, it is said, 'asks more questions and gets more answers'. He certainly expects a much fuller story than departments will normally supply to MPs. Moreover, complaints taken up by the Parliamentary Commissioner, unlike most of those pursued by MPs with Ministers, are 'elevated' to the very top of the administrative hierarchy and invariably cross the desk of the Permanent Secretary. A department's comments on a Parliamentary Commissioner case, therefore, are not only based upon an internal investigation of a rather different kind from that carried out in response to MPs' inquiries; they also take account of the views of the most senior official in the department, which are not always the same as those of his subordinates.[86]

A further possible objection to the introduction of a two-track investigation process on the part of the Parliamentary Commissioner relates to the value of his 'audit function'. It has been pointed out that although the total number of individual complaints upheld by the Commissioner has been relatively small (because he has investigated relatively few cases), the fact is that 'many thousands of taxpayers, recipients of social services, property owners, automobile licensees etc. have been helped by changes in administrative practices and procedures resulting entirely or in part from the Commissioner's investigation and reports'. The performance of this 'Ombudsmanic function', it is suggested, may be enhanced by the Commissioner's 'exhaustive investigations'.[87] At first sight, it seems to be a persuasive enough line of argument. Effective cures are based upon accurate diagnoses; and accurate diagnoses call for a careful and thorough examination of patients and ailments.

86 See Roy Gregory and Peter Hutchesson, op.cit., pp.152, 368 and 413-4; for further comment from the then Head of the Home Civil Service on this aspect of Parliamentary Commissioner case work, see *Fourth Report from the Select Committee, 1977-78*, Minutes of Evidence, 10 May 1978, Q.143.

87 See William B Gwynn, 'The Ombudsman in Britian: a Qualified Success in Government Reform', *Public Administration*, Summer 1982.

On the other hand, evidence from other Ombudsman systems indicates that the use of informal methods for dealing with complaints need not impair an Ombudsman's effectiveness in the role of administrative critic. An account of the Hawaiian Ombudsman's *modus operandi* suggests that even the briefest of investigations may sometimes result in the revision of a 'poor procedure'.[88] As we have seen, employing 'fast track' arrangements in some cases does not prevent the Northern Ireland Parliamentary Commissioner from concerning himself with 'systemic weaknesses'.[89] And in France the Mediateur, while he 'cannot investigate directly into the administration' and 'has to rely on investigations conducted by the administration itself', has none the less become 'a prime instrument of the new strategy of administrative reform', simply because 'he is in a position to receive much information on administrative malpractices and to mediate between the administration and the public, which is the primary objective behind current administrative reform programs'.[90]

Whether a two-tier system of investigations would prove workable in practice, and whether or not the disadvantages associated with it would outweigh any good it might do in terms of reducing the throughput time of some cases, thereby raising the standing of the Office in the estimation of MPs and increasing the number of cases they refer, must remain a matter of debate and conjecture. There is no suggestion, it should be said, that anything more than a limited proportion of cases admitted for investigation should be singled out for 'stage 1 only' treatment. Reflecting on what might happen to the Parliamentary Commissioner scheme if there were a 'system of direct access', the Head of the Home Civil Service told the Select Committee in May 1978 that 'the whole nature of the Ombudsman's Office would be changed from that of a very high-powered office inquiring into a few relatively complex cases into a vast citizens' advice bureau ...'[91] The public interest, clearly, would not be served by a transformation of that kind, whether brought about by direct access or by the adoption of a less time-consuming investigation process in an effort to deal with one of the causes of MPs' sense of dissatisfaction with the Office.

Some might argue, indeed, that altogether too much emphasis is given in this paper to the views and preoccupations of Members. There is no escaping the fact, however, that it is their attitudes and practices which are central to the success of the Parliamentary Commissioner's operations. If MPs disapprove of the Office or have no confidence in it, clearly they are in a position to ensure

88 See W B Gwyn, 'The Conduct of Ombudsman Investigations of Complaints', in G E Caiden (ed), op.cit., pp.83-4.

89 See above, p.31.

90 See Jacques Menier and Henri Desfeuilles, 'France' in Gerald E Caiden (ed), op.cit., pp.107 and 110.

91 See *Fourth Report from the Select Committee, 1977-78,* Minutes of Evidence, 10 May 1978, Q.143.

that its full potential is not realised. What is less often appreciate distinctive role of MPs as well-informed 'magnets' for the Offi turned to the positive advantage of the Parliamentary Commissioner scheme.

Most Ombudsman systems, it is said, are to some degree under-used.[92] The reason, in part, is no doubt to be found in the problems of making the existence and functions of the Office sufficiently well known in the population at large. But as the Parliamentary Commissioner put it in his Annual Report for 1982, 'the need for 'missionary work' is arguably less in this country than in others where Ombudsmen may take up complaints referred to them directly by the citizen'.[93] No one would seriously suggest that the extent of public awareness of the Office is a matter of no consequence. But because the activities of MPs as 'constituency grievance men' are well established and understood; and because it is open to MPs to refer complaints from aggrieved persons who may be unaware of the Parliamentary Commissioner and his functions, the extent of public as opposed to Parliamentary knowledge of the Office ought not to be anything like as important a problem in the United Kingdom as elsewhere. If the advantages for the Office of having 650 MPs as possible points of contact with the general public are to come into play, however, it is essential that MPs themselves should understand how the Parliamentary Commissioner scheme works and be reasonably well-disposed towards it.

92 See Gerald E Caiden, 'Introduction' in Gerald E Caiden (ed), op.cit., pp.xix-xx.

93 See Parliamentary Commissioner, *Annual Report for 1982*, H.C. 257, 23 March 1983, para. 13.

Chapter 2

A Prison Ombudsman of sorts: The long road to reform

Mick Ryan and Tony Ward

This paper traces the lobby to establish a Prison Ombudsman. Particular attention is given to the proposals of the Woolf Report (1991). These proposals recommended significant changes to prisoners' grievance procedures, but fell well short of the penal lobby's demand for an independent Prison Ombudsman. The government's very recent decision (1993) to establish a Prison Ombudsman, on lines which largely reflect Woolf's recommendations rather than the lobby's original proposals, is reviewed in a critical postscript.

Few academic criminologists or penal lobbyists have much to say in favour of the work done by the Parliamentary Commissioner for Administration, ourselves included. He reports on very few prison cases - 38 between 1984 and 1989 - and invariably finds no evidence of maladministration, simply minor infractions of procedures here and there. All this against a background, for example, of 290,000 landing, wing and governors' complaints by prisoners in 1988, and 14,500 individual prisoner petitions to the Secretary of State.[1] Surely, it is argued, the Commissioner should be more actively involved in dealing with this avalanche of grievances, and procedures which restrict his more active involvement must be swept aside? While there is much lobby support for this line of argument, there are those like Lord Justice Woolf who seek reforms by other means, completely bypassing the widespread demand for enlarging the powers of the PCA, or even more radical, the setting up of a separate Prisons Ombudsman answerable to Parliament, as proposed by the Prison Reform Trust.[2]

The purpose of this paper is to explore these differences, but before doing so it is important to outline prison grievance procedures as they presently exist in order to contextualise the debate surrounding the Ombudsman and his powers.

---

1 Woolf LJ and Judge Steven Tumim, 'Prison disturbances', April 1990 (Cm. 1456, HMSO, 1991) para. 14.317.

2 Submission to Phase 2 of the Woolf Inquiry into Prison Disturbances (Prison Reform Trust, London, 1990), para. 42 (e).

Internal Grievance Procedures

Broadly speaking there are four stages to the internal grievance procedure.

First, prisoners are encouraged to make verbal complaints to their wing officer or manager, which are recorded and are normally taken up on the same day. This is a sensible procedure. Very often the grievances are minor and need go no further than the wing or landing to secure a rapid and acceptable adjudication.

Second, if prisoners cannot obtain satisfaction from those immediately around them they can petition the governor. In many cases the person who investigates the prisoner's complaint is a senior member of prison staff rather than what is referred as the governing Governor. A reply should be sent within seven days.

Third, if the governor's adjudication is felt to be unsatisfactory the prisoner may send his or her complaint to the area office, or on 'reserved subjects' - namely parole, early release and disciplinary adjudications - to headquarters itself. The prisoner can expect to receive a reply within six weeks.

The fourth channel is to appeal to the Board of Visitors. While these Boards now receive some legal support they are mainly made up of part-time lay people from the local community whose task is to oversee the administration of the prison. They are in theory the 'eyes and ears' of the Home Secretary who is responsible to Parliament for all that goes on in our prisons. They have the authority to investigate any grievance or pass it on to the area manager or even the Home Secretary.

The sequence in which these various internal channels can be used by a prisoner is a matter of some dispute. For example, Lord Justice Woolf felt it was unnecessary to insist that all complaints must first be considered by the Governor before they could be formally laid before the Board of Visitors, which was the Prison Department's ruling in 1990.[3] It is also important to note that in recent years, and in order to secure confidentiality, prisoners may make their complaints using a sealed envelope to the Governor, Area manager or Board of Visitors (though again, what this confidentiality amounts to is in dispute).[4]

The underlying weaknesses in the system so far outlined are fairly clear, and to an extent, agreed. In procedures one to three the absence of an independent element is unlikely to secure justice. All that happens, in truth, is that the department investigates itself; and pressure, say, on a Governor to find in favour of his or her staff against prisoners is intense. It is no wonder that prisoners feel the procedure is loaded against them at this level. Indeed the

3 Woolf, op.cit., para. 14.320.

4 *Ibid*, para. 14.325.

impossibility of the Governor's position vis-à-vis *all* parties is well summarised by JUSTICE:

> He suffers from the disadvantage, in the case where the conduct of his subordinate officers is in question, of not being, or not seeming to the prisoner to be, a truly independent tribunal. If he dismisses the complaint, he may be suspected of taking sides with the officers. If he upholds it, his officers may feel that he is undermining their authority.[5]

Similar conflicts of interest necessarily arise when complaints are taken up by area office or headquarters. But what of the Boards of Visitors? Made up of lay persons, they can surely be counted on to be more independent? Regrettably, this is far from being the case, and for a number of reasons.

In the first place, while Boards of Visitors are indeed formally independent, it is nevertheless their statutory duty to work with both the Home Secretary (who appoints them) and with local governors to ensure the smooth running of the prison system. In this sense they view themselves - and prisoners view them likewise - as part of the management team. As a consequence, when complaints about prison rules or questions over their interpretation come before them the Boards of Visitors are reluctant to rock the boat, usually unwilling to upset the Governor or Deputy Governor who sits in on disciplinary proceedings. This management perspective is well articulated by Mike Maguire:

> The direct relationship and responsibility of the Boards to the Home Office and to local governors clearly led many members to feel that they were is some senses 'part of the team', with a stake in the system, working within and accepting its rules and values. Thus a common attitude to applications was that, while one might sympathise with the complainant, it would be wrong to 'interfere with management' by seriously questioning discretionary actions, while the majority felt that questioning the rules was not part of the Boards' function. Generally speaking complaints were viewed as no more than an opportunity for prisoners to 'let off steam' ...[6]

Given this approach to their role, it is hardly surprising that a second and, in our view, well-founded criticism of the Boards is that their adjudications are often cursory and deskbound, too reliant on written staff reports rather than active investigation to get to the bottom of the prisoner's complaint. For these and other reasons the Boards of Visitors are seen as no more independent than channels one to three.

5 Justice in Prison (JUSTICE, London, 1983), para. 50.

6 M Maguire, 'Prison Grievances: The Role of Boards of Visitors', in M Maguire, J Vagg and R Morgan (eds.) *Accountability and Prisons* (London, Tavistock, 1985), p.145.

External Grievance Procedures

In an attempt to secure a more independent investigation of grievances there is at the end of the day nothing to stop prisoners from using outside channels. They might, for example, write to their member of Parliament or contact one of the reform groups, say the Howard League. Such contacts are by no means unusual. Unfortunately neither of these agencies, acting independently, has much clout. The Prison Department might agree to look into the grievance referred to it, but in any event neither lobby groups nor MPs can pursue individual cases to the point of securing an independent investigation and requiring redress. Short of rooftop protests or letters to the press, this leaves prisoners just two other channels, the courts and the Ombudsman.

The courts have intervened in recent years, but only to a limited extent. In broad terms, the courts have taken a 'hands off' approach to the day to day administration of prisons and the prison rules are not seen to confer special rights on prisoners enabling them successfully to sue in the courts for non-compliance, even where the grievance is claimed to be a serious one.[7]

However, the courts have recently intervened in very specific areas, such as the conduct of disciplinary hearings by Boards of Visitors. The landmark case was *St Germain*.[8] Following the Hull prison uprising in 1976 a large number of prisoners were charged with serious disciplinary offences, taken before Boards of Visitors where they were mostly found guilty and given harsh punishments. St Germain and others sought judicial review, arguing that for a number of reasons they were prevented from presenting their cases properly before the Boards and that this amounted to a denial of natural justice. In agreeing to hear their case, and by finding in their favour, the courts established for the first time that this area of prison life at least was within their jurisdiction. This new departure was further consolidated in the case of *Tarrant* (1984),[9] and perhaps it was the intervention of the courts that finally persuaded the government to do away with the disciplinary functions of Boards of Visitors altogether in 1991.[10]

In addition to this very special area of prison life the courts have also acted to protect the rights of prisoners to have reasonable access to lawyers and the courts for other reasons. For example, the European Court of Human Rights ruled in the case of *Golder*[11] that it was improper for the Prison Department

7 See for example *Williams v. Home Office (No.2)* [1981] 1 All ER 1211; *R v. Deputy Governor of Parkhurst Prison, ex parte Hague*, [1991] 3 All ER 733.

8 *R v. Board of Visitors of Hull Prison ex parte St Germain* [1979] 1 All ER 71.

9 *R v. Secretary of State ex parte Tarrant* [1984] 1 All ER 799; [1984] 2 WLR 613.

10 'Custody, care and Justice: The Way Ahead for the Prison Service in England and Wales' (London, HMSO, Cm 1647), Ch. 8.

11 *Golder v. United Kingdom* (1979-80) 1 ECHRR 524.

not to allow a prisoner access to a solicitor for the purpose of taking out a civil action for defamation, in this case, against a prison officer. In the light of this and other cases the British government was taken to task by the European Commission on Human Rights for trying to insist that prisoners must first take their cases through the internal complaints procedure, as outlined above, before applying for redress through the courts.[12]

The legal interventions we have outlined above are not without their drawbacks. There is a tight time limit on seeking judicial review, and to take a case before the European Court of Human rights is both a lengthy and a costly business. Also, and more to the present point, the courts seem only willing to intervene in prison life where cases touch on quasi-judicial proceedings or where prisoners' rights of access to the wider judicial system are being restricted. This leaves much of prison life untouched by the courts.

Intervention by the Ombudsman has also been restricted, as we have already indicated. There are several reasons for this. In the first place, the PCA's terms of reference are to seek out maladministration in the application of prison rules, standing orders, etc., not to consider whether such rules or standing orders are in any way unjust or unfair; although he can point out where this strict application causes undue hardship. This necessarily restricts the type of investigation he can carry out - the Prison Rules, for example, go more or less unchallenged - and consequently bars many complaints. Other would-be complainants are discouraged by the fact that they must first go through their MPs, or if they write directly to the Commissioner, that their MPs must agree to an investigation.[13] Time is also a consideration. The PCA only gets through a handful of prison cases in any given year, and for short and medium term prisoners this timescale is pretty hopeless.[14]

Of course, the Ombudsman does some good; the argument is simply that he could and should do more. As Patrick Birkinshaw has written:

> It could be said that the fact that officials know that the `long-stop' of the PCA exists and that they may have to face searching questions and have any errors made public knowledge by the Parliamentary Select Committee on the PCA, contributes over the long term to more attention being given to the fairness of their procedures. It is also true that he has criticised `extreme' conditions in local prisons and revealed some of the more pettifogging rules on privileges.

---

12 Sir James Fawcett, 'Application of the European Convention on Human Rights' Maguire et al., op.cit., 76.

13 P.Birkinshaw, 'An Ombudsman for Prisons' in Maguire et al., op.cit.

14 While the time taken over each investigation has now been reduced, in the mid-1980s it took the PCA nearly a year to complete each case. Parliamentary Commissioner for Administration, Annual Report, 1986.

However, such achievements are only minor in comparison with the vast range of important issues in which he could become involved, and are anyway offset by the refusal of the PCA to challenge rules made by the Prison Department ...[15]

Like JUSTICE, Birkinshaw calls for

a special ombudsman operating for prisoners, and not simply an extension of the powers of the present PCA to take more account of prisons. Such an office should not be grafted on to that of the PCA because - and here I borrow from models operating outside the UK - a prison ombudsman should have full powers to question the merits of Departmental polices, rules and standing orders and to criticise them openly when they are simply bad. Moreover, there should be no necessity to go through an MP, but access should be direct once the complaint had been raised with the authorities.[16]

We shall not restate all of Birkinshaw's and JUSTICE's arguments here, but it is surely clear from our brief outline of existing grievance procedures that they are far from satisfactory. The internal procedures lack the essential ingredient of independence while external channels are variously lengthy, costly or constrained in their ability to investigate matters which are at the heart of many prisoners' grievances, not least the Prison Rules themselves.

A Prison Complaints Adjudicator and the PCA

Pressure to amend internal grievance procedures has been exerted for some time. In 1975 Lord Jellicoe doubted that boards of visitors could act as fora to hear grievances if they continued to act as disciplinary tribunals.[17] The organisation JUSTICE also questioned the impartiality of boards of visitors in 1983, and recommended several changes to the Prison Rules, including dropping the rule which made it an offence to makes 'any false or malicious allegation against a prison officer'.[18] As a result of these and other pressures, not least from prisoners who bitterly complained about delays in responding to their grievances, the Prison Department set up a working group to review its own internal procedures in 1988.[19] This resulted in the removal of certain restrictions on making complaints, such as the Prison Rule about making false and malicious allegations, and in the suggestion that the entire grievance procedure should be streamlined and operate to a timetable. This new procedure was put into operation in 1990, and it is broadly the one we have

15 Birkinshaw, op.cit., p.170.

16 *Ibid*, p.171.

17 Lord Jellicoe (Chair), Boards of Visitors of Penal Institutions (London, Barry Rose, 1975).

18 JUSTICE, op.cit., p.72, para. 27.

19 Woolf, op.cit., para. 14.315.

outlined in this part of this paper.[20] It is also highly relevant that the working group recommended that once the new procedure was in place consideration should be given to the appointment of an independent Complaints Investigator. It was at this point that Lord Justice Woolf entered the debate.

It will be remembered that apart from investigating the Strangeways and related disturbances in 1990, Woolf LJ interpreted his terms of reference to include an inquiry into the prison system as a whole. His subsequent and wide-ranging report (written in collaboration with Judge Stephen Tumim, HM Chief Inspector of Prisons) stressed the importance of justice, emphasising that nothing is more likely to destabilise the prison system than inmates who feel that they are being unjustly treated on a day to day basis. Given this tone it was hardly surprising that Woolf took a special interest in grievance procedures, and he duly lists (paras. 14.432 - 14.343) all those organisations, including (interestingly) the Association of Members of Boards of Visitors, who proposed the creation of a Prison Ombudsman. The Prison Reform Trust was characteristically blunt, demanding that an Ombudsman `with a broad remit, not just maladministration, should be appointed forthwith.' But in spite of strong pressure from what was a well organised lobby, Woolf LJ. had other ideas. What were these? Why did he reject the idea of a Prison Ombudsman? And are they acceptable? It is to these questions that we now turn.

To begin at a very basic level, what Woolf recommended was the appointment of an independent Complaints Adjudicator whose role would be to `recommend, advise and conciliate' (para. 14.349). The Adjudicator would be appointed by, and answerable only to, the Home Secretary. His or her services could be called upon once the prisoner had exhausted all other `internal' channels, such as appeals to the governor, the area manager or even, in `reserved' subjects, headquarters. According to Woolf, the appointment of a suitably efficient, independently-minded Adjudicator would render the idea of a separate Prison Ombudsman redundant (para. 14.351). As for the role of the PCA, the report concludes:

> We considered particularly whether an Adjudicator on these lines makes otiose an application to the Parliamentary Commissioner for Administration in respect of maladministration. We have been grateful for evidence from and a most informative discussion with the Parliamentary Commissioner ... To close the avenue to the Parliamentary Commissioner would require amending legislation. We do not believe that such an avenue should be closed. It should still be possible for prisoners to complain through a Member of Parliament to the Commissioner when they believe that the Prison Service has been guilty of maladministration..' (para. 14.353)

20 The available evidence suggests that these new procedures failed miserably. A Parliamentary question in 1992 revealed that almost one in three of prisoners' requests and complaints to area managers were not dealt within the time limit set by the Prison Department (Prison Report no. 21, Winter 1992, p.11).

According to this formula then, prisoners would retain their existing right to apply to the PCA through their MP as well as securing the new right to appeal to the Prison Complaints Adjudicator.

It is difficult to be certain why Woolf LJ rejected the lobby's call for a Prison Ombudsman, as no *reasoned* argument is made out in the final report except for the somewhat circular one that an independent and efficient Adjudicator would make one unnecessary (see above). We are inclined to believe that the real reasons behind his choice were political ones. To start with, the massive changes recommended, in what was after all a highly damning report, were sold to the Home Secretary on the basis that many of the reforms already reflected official thinking. And in the case of reforming grievance procedures this was certainly true. The idea of a Complaints Investigator had already been floated. It was therefore easy for the government to say in its response to the Report in the White Paper, 'Custody, Care and Justice', that it was indeed genuinely 'attracted' to the idea of a Complaints Adjudicator.[21] Second, the prison system was still in shock after Strangeways and there was a feeling that swift action was necessary. Thus, those reforms, and there were many as the lobby freely pointed out, that could be implemented without the need for primary legislation were most likely to get the green light. On this basis, too, the Complaints Adjudicator was a better bet.

We may all agree, of course, that there is nothing wrong with such pragmatism provided the Complaints Adjudicator can indeed do what the penal lobby had previously believed could only be done by a reformed PCA or Prisons Ombudsman. But is this the case, or has meaningful reform been shelved? It is difficult to be sure - a lot will depend on how the Adjudicator works out in practice - but the omens are not altogether encouraging.

In the first place the Adjudicator may be, like the recently appointed Chief Inspector of Prisons, technically independent of the Prison Department, but he or she is to be likewise appointed by, and directly answerable to, the Home Secretary. We acknowledge that there are degrees of independence, and that a legally trained Adjudicator is likely to be more of his or her own person than a career civil servant from the Prison Department. Nonetheless, we would argue that what on is on offer, and what the government is apparently willing to accept, is more a strengthening of *internal* grievance procedures than a contribution to enlarging external accountability, which is what is really needed.

The second worry is that the Adjudicator's terms of reference may turn out to be too restrictive. The government has so far (1992) not declared its hand on this crucial issue, but the Woolf Report suggests that the Adjudicator's powers, though apparently wider than those of the existing Ombudsman, will be significantly narrower than those of the Prisons Ombudsman envisaged by reformers. In three paragraphs of conflicting signals Woolf argues:

21 'Custody, Care, and Justice', op.cit., p.93.

> 14.357 The Complaints Adjudicator ... would be concerned both with the merits of the complaint and with the manner in which the decision giving rise to the grievance had been considered ...
>
> 14.360 It would not be part of the Complaints Adjudicator's role to determine what should be the policy of the Prison Service with regard to prisoners generally. His concern would be with individual grievances and how they were handled by the Prison Service.
>
> 14.361 This may be a particular concern in relation to prison rules and Regulations and `reserved' subjects. So far as these matters are concerned, we would prefer there to be no special restriction placed upon the jurisdiction of the Complaints Adjudicator. However in practice, we would not expect the Complaints Adjudicator to make recommendations which conflicted with decisions on the merits by Headquarters. He would regard his role in such cases as being a supervisory role. It would be similar to that performed by the High Court in judicial review, a role which primarily involves scrutinising the decision making process.

These remarks are not a model of precision, but it does appear that some advance on the Ombudsman's powers is involved. Like the Ombudsman, the Complaints Adjudicator will not, it seems, be able to question Prison Rules, Standing Orders or *policy* decisions; but unlike the Ombudsman, he or she will be permitted to criticise discretionary decisions in *individual cases* (other than those on reserved subjects) even though the decisions are reached without maladministration.[22] In other words, the Complaints Adjudicator could, in principle, substitute his or her judgment for that of the decision-maker in individual cases. How often the Adjudicator will wish to do this in practice is another matter. The Adjudicator will have only limited investigative resources[23] and in many cases may well feel - not unreasonably - that the man or woman on the spot is in the best position to make a judgment.

What is clear is that by excluding Prison Rules, Standing Orders and policy questions from the Adjudicator's remit, Woolf's proposal falls well short of the wide-ranging powers of the Prison Ombudsman that the lobby were hoping for. Moreover, on the question of 'reserved subjects', the government's response has been even more restrictive than envisaged by Woolf. Parole decisions are firmly excluded from the ambit of the Complaints Adjudicator, and the White Paper indicates that there may even be other `areas which it would not be appropriate to refer to such a body.'[24]

A further cause for concern is that the Complaints Adjudicator will also act as a final `court of appeal' in disciplinary proceedings. It seems ironic that

22 cf. *R v. Local Commissioner for Administration ex Parte Bradford City Council* [1979] 2 All ER 881.

23 'about three assistant adjudicators' and secretarial support: Woolf, para. 14.354. (But see Postscript.)

24 Custody, Care and Justice, para. 8.8. (See Postscript).

the Woolf Report, having acknowledged the need to separate the disciplinary and `watchdog' functions of Boards of Visitors, should combine these same two functions in the new Complaints Adjudicator. The danger, as with Boards of Visitors, is that one function will undermine prisoners' confidence in the other. This danger is compounded by the peculiar nature of the proposed appellate procedure. Rather than holding a formal hearing to decide whether to overturn a governor's adjudication, 'The Adjudicator would be able to see reports from the Area Manager, the governor, the Boards of Visitors and the prisoner, and normally talk to the parties if he so wished' (para. 14.425). But would the prisoner have the right to see these reports, or be present at these conversations? Apparently not. This looks to us - and is likely to look to prisoners - like a denial of natural justice.[25] Nor is prisoners' confidence in the appeal system likely to be enhanced by the fact that they will have no right to legal representation (although there would be a discretion to allow it) and in the absence of a lawyer will have the choice between representation by a fellow prisoner or a prison officer acting `impartially as a friend of the prisoner' (para. 14.441). If prisoners' confidence in the appellate procedure is undermined by these deficiencies, their confidence in the Complaints Adjudicator as an arbitrator of grievances will surely fall with it.

We are inclined to believe that for this reason, as well as the fact the adjudicator is to be directly answerable to the head of the prison service, the Home Secretary, that complaints to the existing Ombudsman will still be forthcoming. For all his or her faults, he or she may well be seen as more independent than the Adjudicator.

A Just Prison?

The final point we wish to raise is one which suggests to us that not only Woolf's proposal for a Complaints Adjudicator, but his whole notion of a `just prison' is fundamentally flawed. In a remarkable display of unanimity, the National Prisoners' Movement,[26] the Prison Officers' Association and the Prison Service all drew attention to the fact that alongside the formal disciplinary procedure in prisons there exists an `informal' or `underground' system based on such measures as segregation in the interests of good order and discipline (Rule 43) and transfers of `disruptive' prisoners between institutions (Circular Instruction 37/1990). The Report concludes - albeit with some reluctance - that these procedures must be retained (paras. 12.221 - 12.296). To the Prison Service's frank admission that these measures could undermine any

25 Natural justice requires that prisoners should know of any evidence that is prejudicial to them and have the opportunity to contradict it (*Board of Education v.* [1911] AC 179; *Kanda v. Government of Malaya* [1962] AC 322; *R v. Parole Board and Another Ex parte Wilson* (1992) The Independent, 5 February). The proposed procedure will, at best, be open to the suspicion that the adjudicator may have given prejudicial information without the appellant's knowledge.

26 In the person of Mr Geoff Coggan (quoted at para. 14.432).

reforms of the formal disciplinary system, since `The punishments available at an adjudication are by no means the only sanctions available to Governors' (para. 14.433), Woolf can respond only with a semantic quibble[27] -

> The Prison Service is under a misapprehension to describe these as sanctions. They are, or should be, used only as necessary and as specific responses to the actions of prisoners (para. 14.434)

- and by invoking the Complaints Adjudicator:

> The best protection against underground sanctions is to require and expect the Prison Service at all levels to consider its decisions and to give the prisoner reasons for them. If the prisoner is not satisfied, he may then activate the complaints procedure (para. 14.435).

In the case of transfers, CI 37/1990 already requires reasons to be given, so the only additional safeguard proposed by Woolf is the appeal to the Complaints Adjudicator. No doubt some form of external scrutiny is better than none; and decisions of this type could, in principle, be criticised on their merits by the Adjudicator. But even if the Adjudicator does prove capable of unravelling the often unsatisfactory evidence on which such decisions are based,[28] a review which takes place only after the prisoner has exhausted internal complaints procedures will come too late to be of any practical value in many cases - for example, those of short-term 'cooling off' transfers to local prisons. Professor Roy King - whose work with Katherine McDermott shows clearly that disciplinary transfers are in practice seen as punishments by both prisoners and staff[29] - made proposals to the Woolf inquiry designed to inject some procedural justice into the working of CI 37/1990, but these were rejected (paras. 12.255 - 12.257). While King's proposals were not without their difficulties - particularly in the role they envisaged for the Board of Visitors (para. 12.257) - the Complaints Adjudicator proposal falls well short of the degree of external accountability which he rightly sought to achieve.

The Complaints Adjudicator is Woolf's response to the fundamental contradiction of the prison system: that between the ideal of legal justice which the prison symbolises, and the discretionary, disciplinary power on which its administration ultimately depends. As such, it is in our submission manifestly inadequate. A Prisons Ombudsman on the lines proposed by Birkinshaw would not solve the problem either, but would at least be able to tackle it on the level of policy and not merely on a case-by-case basis.

---

27 We do not deny that there is a real distinction here. A sanction, to a lawyer, connotes a coercive measure imposed on someone who has broken a rule. But `underground' measures, as Woolf points out (para. 12.255) can be imposed even where no rule has been broken. Far from defusing the concern expressed by critics, this point underlines it.

28 R King and K McDermott, 'My Geranium is Subversive' (1990) Br. J. Sociol. 41(4): 445-71.

29 *Ibid.*

Conclusion

Our purpose in raising the question of the Ombudsman and the prison system at this time is twofold. First, and most obviously, the Woolf report has put the idea of justice in our prisons at the top of the reform agenda, and some changes to secure the better redress of prisoners' grievances are clearly on their way. Discussion of these changes at a forum such as this is thus desirable. But second, and arguably more important, is our anxiety that Ombudsman studies in the United Kingdom may have been less sympathetic to the plight of prisoners than is reasonably justified. This is not to say that their special vulnerability to administrative injustice is never mentioned, though sometimes this has been the case, but more that this sensibility is often limited by the suggestion that as a group of citizens - and we use the term citizens deliberately - they are more prone to complain than others; that they clog up complaints procedures because they have too much time on their hands, or that they somehow enjoy the attention which complaints attract.[30] Such an attitude, in our view, not only does less than justice to most prisoners, it also serves to block more reasoned argument about the limits of existing procedures and how they might be changed.

Postscript

In January 1993 the Home Office announced the decision to appoint a `Prisons Ombudsman'.[31] Despite the title, the proposed post is virtually identical to that of the `Prison Complaints Commissioner' discussed in our paper. The Home Office makes clear that the Prisons Ombudsman will be able to deal with the merits of individual prisoners' complaints, and that it has decided against excluding certain categories of cases, such as those of Category A (high security risk) prisoners, from the Ombudsman's remit. The Home Office expects the Ombudsman to have a considerable workload - 1700 complaints a year `could be a modest assessment' - and to cope with this they have allowed rather more generous administrative support than Woolf suggested: three Assistant Ombudsmen and nine additional staff.

On the difficult question of appeals from disciplinary proceedings, the Home Office states that the Prisons Ombudsman 'will have no statutory power to rehear a disciplinary case, but should nevertheless be able to review cases on their merits as well as on procedural grounds, on the basis of the documentation available, supplemented by interviews as necessary'. On these as in all other matters, the Prisons Ombudsman's sole power will be to make a

30 R Gregory and P Hutchesson make reference to such attitudes in *The Parliamentary Ombudsman* (Allen & Unwin, 1975), Chapter 13.

31 'Establishing a Prison Ombudsman: A Note on Arrangements', Home Office, Prison Service, 1993.

recommendation addressed to the Chief Executive of the Prison Service. The Government has not followed Woolf's view that `It is right, and consistent with the principles of justice, that an independent element should be able to review and set aside findings which result in a prisoner staying in prison longer than would otherwise be the case' (para. 14.426). Rather than the procedurally flawed appeals system criticised above, we have something that is not really an appeals procedure at all, but a form of administrative review of a quasi-judicial decision.

Apart from this, it is welcome news that Woolf's proposals have not been watered down by the Home Office. It is still the case, however, that these proposals are a significantly watered-down version of the Prisons Ombudsman that the penal lobby had hoped for. Just how serious the shortcomings in the Prison Ombudsman's remit, independence, and ability to deal with disciplinary matters will prove in practice remains to be seen.

Chapter 3

Making bricks without straw: The Polish Ombudsman and the transition to democracy

Howard Elcock

The Ombudsman was invented by the Swedes in their 1809 Constitution. He was originally an instrument for Parliament to use to check on improper Government influence over civil servants but has become an investigator of citizens' complaints.[1] Since 1950, when Denmark established its Ombudsman, the office has spread all over the world.[2] The office is that of an investigator of complaints by citizens against public officials and increasingly private companies, for example in Britain we now have Ombudsmen to investigate complaints against insurance firms and banks.

The spread of the Ombudsman concept across the world has led to its application in a wide range of Constitutions, political and administrative systems, with the result that the institution itself varies widely in its scope, powers and functions in differing countries.[3] Its spread throughout the Western world has been followed by its adoption in one East European state, Poland, as part initially of the development of the Rule of Law along the lines of the European Napoleonic tradition of the enforcement of codes of law on administrators. Under this legal tradition, officials who formerly were not subject to any effective legal control must now accept as binding the provisions of the law which govern their work.[4] The election of the Eastern bloc's first non-Communist Government in Poland in June 1989 was followed by a rapid, often chaotic shift towards a liberal-democratic Constitution, culminating in the holding of Poland's first fully free elections in 1991.

This process of political development has had to be accompanied by a very rapid change in the administrative substructure, from a monolithic apparatus dominated by the Polish United Workers' Party (PZPR) and its two small partners (the Liberal Party and the Peasants' Party), through the emergence, suppression and subsequent re-emergence of the Solidarity trade union, leading up to the establishment of multi-party democracy.[5] Many civil servants and other public administrators have remained in office throughout this period of tumultuous change. Hence, they have had to adapt to the

---

1 N Elder, *Government in Sweden: The Executive at Work* (Pergamon Press, 1970).

2 DC Rowat (ed.), *The Ombudsman: Citizen's Defender* (Allen and Unwin, 1965).

3 F Stacey, *Ombudsmen Compared* (Oxford University Press, 1978).

4 L Garlicki, 'Polish Constitutional Developments in 1980' in WM Butler (ed.), *Anglo-Polish Essays* (New York, 1982).

5 G Kolanciewicz and PG Lewis, *Poland: Politics, Economics and Society* (Pinter Publishers, 1988).

changing demands imposed on them first by the Solidarity Government elected in 1989 and then by the multi-party legislature and government which has resulted from the 1991 elections.

The development of Western-style multi-party politics has been accompanied by the development of a legal system in which the Rule of Law is enforced impersonally by the Courts and other legal officials, instead of the law being subject to the dictates of the PZPR Party 'Line'.[6] Reform of administrative law pre-dated the democratic revolution. Before 1980, 'the judicial review of administrative decisions did not exist in Poland, save certain categories of cases.'[7] However, in 1981 the Sejm vested the judicial branch with 'the power to review the legality of administrative decisions.'[8] and in 1986 the High Administrative Court was supplemented by the creation of a Constitutional Court, with power to review not only administrative decisions but also the constitutionality of regulations and Acts of Parliament.[9] Hence, 'presently, judicial review of administrative decisions plays an important role and gradually is gaining recognition and support in East European countries.'[10]

These reforms were followed on 15th April 1987 by the passage through the Sejm of the Act creating the Polish Ombudsman, the Commissioner for Civil Rights Protection. The first Commissioner, Ewa Letowska, formerly Professor of Civil Law at the University of Warsaw, was appointed in November of that year. Her office opened for the receipt of complaints on 1st January 1988. The Commissioner has now issued three Annual Reports, on which much of the discussion in the rest of this paper is based. The Reports contain a fairly brief statement of information and developments during the year in question, followed by a series of specimen cases dealt with during the year. Table 1 (see page 53) presents some basic statistical information drawn from the most recent available Report, for the year 1990.

Several points need to be made about these figures. First, the initial demand for investigations was huge because there was no time bar (some complaints submitted date back to the 1920s) and the range of authorities subject to the Commissioner's investigation is very large. The level of letters received and petitions submitted has declined but continues at a very high level by international standards (the Commissioner compares her case load with the Swedish case load of 3,456, the French Mediateur's 4,316 cases and the Spanish Ombudsman's total of 3,797 cases[11]). Secondly, 85 per cent of cases

6 L Garlicki, 1982, op.cit. and 'Constitutional and Administrative Courts as Custodians of the State Constitutions: The Experience of East European Countries', *Tulane Law Review*, 1978, Vol. 61, pp.1285-1306.

7 L Garlicki, 1982, op.cit., p.156.

8 *Ibid*, p.157.

9 L Garlicki, 1987, op.cit., p.1296.

10 *Ibid*, p.1304.

11 Annual Report 1990, p.5

Table 1

	1990	1989	1988
Number of letters received	22764	29031	52867
Number of Petitions	18114	17895	44936
Number of Cases completed	3748	3311	1015
Number Pending	3353	-	-
Number of Staff (Full time equivalents)	78	75	55.5

SOURCE: Annual Report 1990, paras. 1 and 2c, p.5

are rejected as not falling within the Commissioner's competence[12] - again a common phenomenon, especially for new Ombudsmen.[13] In 1989-90 the Scottish Local Commissioner for Administration rejected nearly 80 per cent of the complaints submitted to him although his office had then existed for some ten years. The trend in rejected complaints was somewhat upwards.[14] Thirdly, although the Commissioner's staff has steadily increased, shortage of staff is identified by her as a major reason for delays in investigating the 15 per cent of cases that have been accepted as falling within her competence.[15]

We can explore more specific issues identified in the Commissioner's reports under five main headings:

(i) The limits of citizens' comprehension of what matters are and are not appropriate for an Ombudsman to investigate.

(ii) Officials' ignorance of, and reluctance to, accept the Commissioner's (or even the Courts') judgments that they have infringed legal requirements and must make amends.

(iii) The Commissioner's relationship with the legal system.

(iv) The Commissioner's relationship with the higher Courts.

(v) The need to accept that liberal-democracy requires the state to protect minority rights as well as carrying out the expressed will of the majority.

The Public

The citizens of East European countries have not been accustomed to making independent political, social and economic choices and having to abide by the consequences of the choices they make. Furthermore, in the former Communist regimes there was a tradition of writing to 'Letters Bureaux' about all forms of complaint about the activities of the State. However, these letters, although very large in number, had little effect.[16] The Polish Ombudsman commented in 1988 that these Letters Bureaux 'have no authority and their operation is limited to sending the letters to those accused of fault. A complaint has, thus, become trivial, lost its power both with the

12 *Ibid*, para. 2c and d, pp.5-6.

13 F Stacey, *The British Ombudsman* (Oxford University Press, 1971); CM Chinkin and RJ Bailey, 'The Local Ombudsman', *Public Administration*, 1976, Vol. 54, pp.267-282.

14 K Thompson, 'The Office of Commissioner for Local Administration in Scotland: A Socio-Legal Study of its Nature and Effectiveness', CNAA PhD Thesis, Glasgow Polytechnic, 1991, p.59, table 29.

15 Annual Reports of the Commissioner for Civil Rights Protection (English Language Summaries) for 1988, 1989, 1990, published by the Commissioner's Office.

16 M Fainsoch, *How Russia is Ruled*, (2nd ed.) (Oxford University Press, 1963); Kolanciewicz and Lewis, 1988, op.cit.; Annual Report 1988, p.8, para. III:2.

author and the recipient. Therefore the Ombudsman is expected to react more rapidly ...').[17] In a lecture delivered in 1990, Professor Letowska described Polish society as being 'paternalistically demoralised.'[18] Hence, 'one should not wonder that the representatives of the paternalistically demoralised society are deaf to the argument, 'law does not allow' as not the law is important but one's own interests ...'.[19] She started with a very high level of public esteem; only the judges and the Solidarity union were held in higher public regard than the Commissioner, according to an opinion poll taken in 1988.[20] In consequence, the Commissioner receives a very wide range of complaints about such matters as the government's economic policy, the spoiliation of the environment, land reform and housing policy, over which she has no power to intervene.[21] However, such experiences are not uncommon among Ombudsmen in the West.[22]

Officials

Many State and local officials have continued in office during the period of transition to democracy and their attitudes to political change have varied often from the uninformed to outright opposition. 'Conservative cadres' within the PZPR, for example, resisted judicial review of administrative decisions by the High Administrative Court.[23] The reluctance of officials to adapt, or their failure to recognise the need to adapt, to an administrative system in which laws have to be obeyed rather than officials exercising their personal discretion whose use and abuse was protected by the *Nomenklatura* system, is noted frequently by the Commissioner. Also they find it hard to accept that aggrieved citizens are entitled to remedies against official incompetence or misdeeds. This has been not the least of the problems encountered by the Polish Ombudsman. In the lecture quoted earlier, Professor Letowska declared that officials have 'a tendency to purely menial treatment of the law ... In consequence the law is reduced to the role of a 'security document' of a professionally under-educated officer, aware neither of the fact that he himself is a servant of the law, nor that what he considers to

---

17 *Ibid.*

18 Lecture of Professor Dr Ewa Letowska, Commissioner for Civil Rights Protection: 'Ombudsman Institution in Europe: Similarities and Differences, Polish Experience'.

19 *Ibid,* pp.5-6.

20 Interview with Dr Lab Miroslaw Wyrzykowski, Chief of Constitutional Rights and Civil Liberties Department, Office of the Commissioner for Civil Rights Protection, Warsaw, June 1989; H Elcock, 'Working for Socialist Legality: The Polish Commissioner for Citizens' Rights', *Public Policy and Administration,* p.44, Vol. 5, No. 3.

21 Annual Reports of the Commissioner for Civil Rights Protection (English Language Summaries), op.cit.

22 F Stacey, 1971, op.cit.

23 L Garlicki, 1982, op.cit.

be law, is only a weak shadow of what it may be in a legal state.'[24] Officials frequently, it seems, receive the Commissioner's criticisms of their infringements of laws and regulations with surprise and indignation.

The Legal System

Unlike the British Ombudsmen, who are given the remit of investigating complaints of maladministration resulting in injustice - a vague, indeed arguably vacuous definition of their remit [25]and whose conclusions cannot be enforced at law, the Polish Commissioner is specifically charged with investigating administrative acts which are illegal. In this regard, the Commissioner's role is similar to that of Ombudsmen in other Continental European countries where the office is concerned with the application of the legal codes to individual cases.[26] In her report to the Sejm in 1990, the Commissioner declared that 'In matters related to the guarantees of man's economic and social rights, the Commissioner only intervenes if they involve defects in the legal regulations.'[27] Hence, she is dependent on all concerned accepting a positivist view of the status of law - the acceptance that the laws in force must be impersonally enforced - which comes as a novelty to many Polish administrators. The Commissioner's own positivist view is reflected in her ruling that complaints can only be addressed in terms of the law that was in force at the time the decision complained about was made however defective it may, by current standards, have been. In the general level of officials' observance of the law, the Commissioner detected 'no improvement whatever ... so far'[28] which suggests that one of the common benefits of introducing an Ombudsman - an improvement in the conduct of public officials - has yet to materialise in Poland. Also, the Commissioner's positivist acceptance of the existing state of the law and its condition prevailing at the time that events complained of occurred may have caused her to be a disappointment to reformers who see her activity 'on behalf of sanitation of the law' as being 'for all kinds of reformers, too modest ... The reformers do not realise that they tend to make the Ombudsman account for their own tendencies and programmes.'[29] However, unlike the British Ombudsmen, the Commissioner can seek the enforcement of her judgments in the higher administrative courts.

---

24 Lecture of Professor Dr Wea Letowska, op.cit.

25 G Marshall, 'Maladministration', *Public Law*, pp.32-44.

26 N Elder, 1970, op.cit., p.171ff; DC Rowat, 1965, op.cit.; F Stacey, 1978, op.cit.

27 Pronouncement of the Commissioner for Civil Rights Protection prepared for a Session of the Diet of Republic of Poland, on the occasion of the presentration of her Report for the year 1990, p.10.

28 *Ibid*, p.11.

29 Lecture of Professor Dr Ewa Letowska, op.cit., p.9.

The Courts

The Commissioner has now referred several complaints for arbitration by the Constitutional Tribunal. Two recent examples have been cases involving the introduction of religious education in schools and abortion. In a country where 90 per cent of the population are Roman Catholic and where the Church stood as a bulwark resisting Communist oppression for over 40 years, both these issues are obviously of great moral and social significance. In both, the Commissioner took a relatively liberal stance which was not upheld by the Constitutional Court. In the religious education case, the Commissioner argued that making provision for religious education in the state schools constituted an infringement of the secular nature of the State and also that it infringed citizens' rights to privacy because parents and pupils opting into or out of religious education classes would have to reveal their religious beliefs or non-belief. The Constitutional Court, however, argued that religious education classes were not an infringement of citizens' liberties so long as they were voluntary and completely separate from the rest of the school curriculum. In the abortion case, a doctor had refused to issue a statement of reasons to enable a woman to have an abortion, which is permitted under Polish law where a doctor certifies that the patient's health is in danger or that her economic and social circumstances are such that she should not have the baby. The Court, however, upheld the doctor's right to refuse to grant such a certificate on grounds of freedom of conscience. The Commissioner's cases have hence helped to clarify Polish law but have not necessarily produced the results the Commissioner or the complainants sought. It is, of course, of great importance in assessing the effectiveness of such offices as that of Ombudsman, to acknowledge that general benefits such as the clarification of the law or the improvement of administrators' conduct, may result from the Ombudsman's actions, even if the complainant loses his or her case.[30]

Minority Rights

The ideology of Marxism-Leninism assumes that where a State has achieved Socialism, there are no social conflicts because all class conflict has ceased. In consequence, there is no need to protect minority rights. In liberal-democracies, by contrast, the protection of minority rights is an essential prerequisite of democratic government.[31] The office of Ombudsman has a role in ensuring the protection of minority rights. Professor Letowska has declared

30 G Marshall, 1973, op.cit.
31 See JS Mill, various.

that: 'The ... populist trend of democracy considers the minority to be wrong just because it is less numerous. The other liberal one where politics are aimed at co-ordination of different interests; the majority's priority is by no means tantamount to disregard of the minority interests.'[32] Hence, 'It is the Commissioner's task to see to a proper use of law which should be in accordance with the requirements of professionalism and honesty and not instrumental.'[33] The Commissioner also sees it as her duty to ensure that Polish administrators comply with the demands of international guarantees of human rights.

This short paper has demonstrated that the Polish Commissioner for Civil Rights Protection has encountered many problems which Ombudsmen in other countries have also had to face. Equally, there are some distinctive issues which arise from the former Communist system and which have to be resolved as part of the transition from the Marxist- Leninist one-party state to the establishment of a pluralist, multi- party democracy. The Ombudsman is a curiously loosely-defined office which has been applied in a wide range of Constitutional settings; the Polish version of the office has produced particular dilemmas arising from the inevitably slow and difficult process of replacing the old Communist certainties with stable and securely established democratic State and legal systems.

References

Note

I am indebted to Professor Leszek Garlicki, of the Faculty of Law and Administration, University of Warsaw, for his kind help and hospitality on my visits to Poland in May 1987 and June 1989 and to Dr Hab Miroslaw Wyrzykowski for granting me an extended interview in Warsaw in June 1989.

32 Pronouncement of the Commissioner for Civil Rights Protection, op.cit.

33 *Ibid*, p.23.

Chapter 4

The Bedfordshire Ombudsperson: The first six months

Elizabeth Hodder

The decision by Bedfordshire County Council to have an Ombudsperson was taken more than eighteen months ago. It was viewed as a public statement of the Council's commitment to extend the rights of the citizen in Bedfordshire. The appointment received enthusiastic support from the Labour and Social Liberal Democrat groups, who viewed the role as an extension of the opportunities available to priority clients to make their voice heard within the Council. Part of the enthusiasm arose from the debate surrounding the mandatory introduction of a complaints system for the Social Services Department in April 1991. The post was not without its controversy. Certainly the Conservative Group (the largest group in a County where there is no overall political control), whilst supporting the establishment of the post, expressed some concern about possible duplication of their role as the people's representative and an unnecessary tier between the Council and the Local Government Ombudsman. These were criticisms voiced publicly at the time. As the role has since been clarified and as the debate about the citizens charter has become more integral to the political debate of all parties, there seems to be a general acceptance of the value of having an Ombudsperson within County Hall, although the reasons for seeing it as a 'good thing' may differ widely.

I have been in post for just six months and I should like to give a flavour of that time in this talk; but in doing so I should like to focus on matters of more general concern, and, I hope, interest. The first of these concerns the nature of my title - and here I am not referring to the word Ombudsperson - something which is frequently commented on locally but which is largely a matter for Bedfordshire County Council. I mean the word Ombudsman. Have I any right to be known as such when I have no backing in Law, when I am not a Lawyer and find the concept of maladministration as confusing as anyone else and, most important of all, when I am paid by and housed by the same organisation against whom I am meant to find fault. Naturally there is some concern among those who have all of these basic pre-requirements together with a more robust and flexible funding base. If Bedfordshire County Council can give itself one of these beasts then how long will it be before Little Wimblington Parish Council succumbs with the incumbent working part-time on an honorarium of £500 a year? Some of this sensitivity must stem from the very different definitions of the word Ombudsman. The most quoted definition is that of 'Legal Representative' - someone who can extend the rights of the citizen through the processes of law. Not surprisingly, therefore, all such Ombudsmen are well-qualified, well-established and often very well-known Lawyers whose interpretation of a problem brought to them by the citizen depends on this legal knowledge.

Fortunately I am not bound by such a definition - I am tied to the Oxford Dictionary definition of the word - 'People's Defender'. Such a definition allows the widest possible interpretation of the role and opens new doors for both the public and the work of an Ombudsman. It also removes any problems about correct interpretation of the case being brought. I am the voice of the layman (layperson) with a body of 'inside knowledge' and a brief to let the people's voice be heard. What an Ombudsman is there to do is to facilitate, to inform and to mediate as well as to pronounce. This is a completely different interpretation and one which is particularly apt when talking about local government. For the greatest problem local government faces is not that it provides a bad service, but that the public is clueless about the services it provides, who is paying for these services and how they might influence the manner in which these services are delivered. As Bedfordshire's Ombudsman I can help encourage the public's voice to be heard more loudly and, by keeping them informed on a global and personal level, can let them know that attention has been paid to their views and that changes will take place as a result.

To some extent this interpretation of the role is my own, reflecting, as it does, a background outside local government working in consumer organisations and having a view about how local government is perceived. The County Council is beginning to put itself in the shoes of the public. I should like to expand on this and describe how the public has used me during these first six months.

When I joined there was a perception that the public were queuing up to complain - that they were unhappy about what we did and, most important of all, that we were not good at handling their complaints. This has not proved to be the case. The public's overriding priority seems to be a need for better information about who does what and where. There was no backlog of disgruntled, mistreated complainants other than those who were already on stream for the Local Government Ombudsman. But there was a large number of people who were confused about the services that were provided and sought help and guidance as to whom they wanted to talk to. So, in these first few months, more than half the enquiries (only some of them are complaints) have nothing to do with the County Council - that is, with what we see the County Council as being there to do. Dogs, drains, divorce and dustbins are as common as sewers, special needs and school transport. This is a problem for all Ombudsmen - the fact that the public will get in touch when they really ought to be contacting someone else, such as a citizens advice bureau or their therapist. But it also shows a very positive trust in someone with the title - the fact that they think they will deal with anything. In the case of local government it reflects the lack of a clear message, a clear financial accountability and the distortion of both of these by the involvement of local councillors. So, should I have deflected all non-county council queries when they arrived on my desk? Or should I accept responsibility for part of the confusion that had led them to me in the first place and help them pursue their problem? As I was new I chose to do the latter, partly because I felt sorry for the public, partly as a means of my learning a lot about who did what in the County and partly because the County's image was at stake. If, as a result of introducing a well-publicised complaints procedure all we could do was to turn people away, then we were sending out a conflicting and negative message to the public. As I have gained more experience I have realised that the confusion of the public is also combined with a general, and somewhat surprising belief that the County Council has control over everything that works within the county. This includes all the District Councils, hospitals, lawyers, etc. The implication, therefore, is that a County Council Ombudsperson is in post not just to deal with County Council complaints but to sort out anything that might be going wrong with the county. This presumes a level of information and contacts that are beyond anyone's reach - also a level of co-operation between the different agencies, particularly of each other's policies which just isn't there on the ground. But in an ideal world is there any reason why an Ombudsman should not have a geographical as opposed to a legal or service boundary?

This was not how my role was envisaged. Before I came to Bedfordshire I had been preceded by Brian Hackland, who was seconded from The Local Government Ombudsman's Office and who planned the complaints procedure in painstaking detail. The package depended upon a commitment from all Departments, which in some cases meant the abandoning of existing complaints procedures. The principle behind the scheme, and one which is universal, is that, wherever possible, the complainant receives satisfaction from the person who provided the service. In the rare instances where this was not going to be possible then a full investigation would be conducted using the approach adopted by the Local Government Ombudsman - that is, the complainant would see copies of any report before it became final. This investigation would be conducted within the relevant Department and overseen by the Departmental Customer Relations Officer - someone who is responsible for the operation of the complaints procedure at all stages. To ensure the maximum independence of such an investigation it may well be necessary to appoint someone from a different section or different geographical location to act as Investigation Officer. So far only one such investigation has occurred: all other complaints have been handled at the first stage - informally, within Departments. This has meant that so far no complaints have reached stage three - which is the one where the OMBUDSPERSON becomes involved either in an investigating capacity or in reviewing the case. Records of all complaints, external and internal, together with all compliments and suggestions are kept by each department for reporting to their own programme committee and on an annual basis to a group of representatives from outside voluntary organisations. The first such departmental reports are being prepared now for the next round of committees. The earlier training and information - sharing in the field of customer care and complaints - handling has fostered a more positive base from which to go public, department by department and also as a united Council.

The theory behind the idea of an internal Ombudsperson is a very good one. The principal value is the deterrent one - that by having someone with a clear investigative brief and a commitment to the public, departments will make every effort to ensure that all complaints are handled as quickly and thoroughly as possible. The fact that all complainants who use our own, widely distributed complaints form reach departments via myself is an added inducement for action to take place. For everyone knows that 'I know' if a complaint has been received and that I have access to the complainant: this is a further incentive for speedy action. The public, too, appears reassured that there is another person within the County Council committed to helping them and on their side against a large 'bureaucracy'.

So what are the conclusions to having such a post and what conclusions can I draw from a very short period of time?

An Ombudsman gives across a very positive message to the public that the services offered by Bedfordshire County Council could, and should be improved. By being readily accessible and turning away nobody, an Ombudsman gives out an unbiased message that we are concerned, not just to improve our services, but also to improve the quality of life in all fields. This requires the willing co-operation of others in the statutory sections and a high profile throughout the county. Having one named individual with a clear role gives courage to those who previously might have failed in pursuing their complaint as a result of being unsure of whom to contact.

However, it also appears that the public's interest in local government and the need to complain about it is never going to be as strong as, say, the services provided by British Rail and British Telecom. Because the public cannot link their bits of money to the services they receive they are not sure whether local government is doing well or badly. This may be another argument for unitary local authorities - one provider of services means one body against whom to complain - so no more buck-passing. But even this would not answer the large number of the public who want to complain to the County Council about their pensions or about the local hospitals. There is some sense in the idea of a geographically-based Ombudsman.

Finally I should say that the Council appears to be providing good services. All that appeared to be required was a confidence that this was so. Through training, sharing of good practice and the introduction of very minor, but far-reaching, changes in the method of delivering these services it has been possible to make a start in convincing both the staff and the public that the Council is committed to making these good services even better.

Chapter 5

The Local Government Ombudsman: Contemporary issues and challenges

F G Laws

The Current Problem

The issue which has overshadowed all others in my Commission has been the growth in business evidenced by the increase in the volume of complaints received. In 1984 (the year I became a Commissioner) the Commission processed 3019 complaints. In the year ended 31 March 1991 the corresponding number was 8714 and in the current year we have already received in excess of 10,000. As a result of this it has been necessary to increase the staff from 56 in 1984 to 115 at the present date. In the like period the budget has grown from £1.2 million in 1984 to an estimated expenditure of £4.9 million in the current year. As a consequence the three Commissioners are now on separate sites - the Commissioner for the North, still in York but in larger officers. I have been transferred to new offices in Coventry and the Commissioner for London remains in Westminster but only whilst new offices are found in the London area to accommodate the enlarged team. Why has all this come about? It would be popular in some circles to say the growth proves the rising inefficiency of local authorities but that would be unfair and untrue. Remarkably for all the growth in complaints received the percentage results of complaints upheld, rejected or settled has remained remarkably constant over the years. In 1984 10 per cent were upheld, 79 per cent were rejected, 11 per cent settled, whereas in 1991 3 per cent were upheld, 80 per cent were rejected and 17 per cent settled. Indeed in the six years 1985-1990 inclusive complaints rejected varied between 74 per cent and 81 per cent of the total received - the balance being either settled voluntarily by the Council, or maladministration was found in a formal report. It may well be that there is now a greater awareness of the availability of the service, and that accounts for part of the growth in volume of complaints. I can however point to one significant factor and that is the actual increase which must be attributable to direct access to the Ombudsman.

When the service was established in 1974 the statute required complaints to be made first to a member of the subject Council and if necessary, then referred on to the Local Government Ombudsman. In May 1988 the law was changed (Local Government Act 1988) and complainants could for the first time communicate their grievance direct to the Ombudsman. Some have always done that of course and to be helpful we were obliged to perform a ritual administrative dance to bring them within jurisdiction. That change in the law brought a 44 per cent increase alone. One might have hoped that a platform had then been reached but it was not to be - the numbers continue upwards and we face a 25 per cent increase this year.

I have to say that our performance has slipped to a maladministrative level during this fairly violent upheaval and only now is the Commission creeping back to an acceptable response time. To be taking four and five months to answer a simple complaint and one and a half years to issue a report is something of which I am ashamed. My only defence is that we are financed from Treasury funds, the Government's policy on public expenditure is well known and the Commission has had to struggle to secure the resources needed.

The Commission's Influence

If we were judged by the number of complaints upheld or grievances settled (3 per cent to 17 per cent respectively last year) one might be tempted to ask whether it was worth the effort. I regret that cynical view because it would deny the nature of the problem. Many of my clients are, to say the least, emotionally disturbed by their experiences and the grievance has sometimes reached obsessional proportions. I believe that even in circumstances where the Ombudsman cannot obtain a remedy a sympathetic ear must have some therapeutic value.

On the other hand the Commission is an influence towards better administration. The Local Government and Housing Act 1989 imposes a positive duty to advise on good practice and we have been working at it so that shortly we will issue our guidance on local complaints procedures and later a variety of other topics. The Ombudsman's reports themselves have precedent value for local authorities - they are public documents and Messrs Longmans now publish a guide which summarises in an updated loose leaf form a string of decisions on a wide variety of topics reviewed by Ombudsmen. I believe we have already considerably influenced the attitude of planning authorities to publicity for planning applications. About 40 per cent of my cases are about planning issues and very often it is the case of a neighbour upset by what the Council has allowed to be done to the property next door. If the neighbour should, in fairness, have been given notice of the planning application so that he could express his views to the Council, but was left in ignorance, then I am likely to be critical. The practice of neighbour notification is now widespread and indeed the Government proposes to amend the Town and Country Planning General Development Order to extend the scope of mandatory notification cases. I think Ombudsmen's strictures on this issue have been heard. There have been other issues. The publicity which followed adverse reports against education authorities who were illegally charging for school trips brought a change in the law.

Many more highway authorities now have a clear policy on dealing with footpath obstructions the 'bete noir' of the Ramblers Association.

I always say where appropriate that Councils should never try to be 'Ombudsman-proof'. However careful they may be, administrative errors will occur and the last thing they should do is nothing for fear of the wrath of the Ombudsman. A local authority association did, not so long ago, recommend Councils not to have a policy on one topic to prevent the Ombudsman being able to find fault. That is foolishness.

Maladministration

As you will know, my role is to investigate injustice caused by maladministration, although neither term is defined in the statute. We still rely on the Crossman catalogue, which is the broad definition of maladministration used by the late Richard Crossman when piloting the Bill through the House of Commons in 1971 - bias neglect inattention delay incompetence ineptitude perversity turpitude and arbitrariness. We are also mindful that this approach was approved by Lord Denning in the application for judicial review by Bradford of a decision by the Commissioner for the North of England in 1979.[1]

He went on to say that 'maladministration' meant what the Ombudsman said it meant, within the broad guide lines, of which he approved and the Ombudsman would be making up the definition as he went along. 'Injustice' is not so difficult a word and the Commissioners interpret that to mean any significant hurt, but it can be interpreted from as little as damaged feelings to material loss. I think that is fine so far as it goes but you will be aware there are statutory limitations on the Ombudsmen's jurisdiction.[2] These exclude for example investigating an employee's complaint against the Council, most contractual and commercial constraints, and the internal management of schools. There are other limitations in that the Ombudsman, unless there are exceptional circumstances, should not investigate complaints when an alternative remedy is available in the Courts or before a statutory tribunal. That is fairly fundamental to an Ombudsman's role and I have no quarrel with it. Other limitations however preclude inquiry into an issue affecting all or most of the inhabitants of the area and specifically prevent the Ombudsman inquiring into the merits of the Council's decision in the absence of maladministration.

As to these limitations, subject to the obvious desirability of not conflicting with other jurisdictions, I feel they are oppressive and unnecessary. If the role of the Ombudsman is accepted as being the duty to investigate administrative

1 *R v. Local Commissioner for Administration in the North and East Area of England, ex parte Bardford* (1979) All ER 881.

2 See the Local Government Act 1974, Sched.5, s.26.

fault causing injustice I see no case for 'no-go' areas. I feel the same about 'all or most' type complaints and I question the provision as to 'merits'. This is probably the source of most grief among complainants than any other limitation because people do see the Ombudsman (wrongly of course) as a court of appeal against unfairness. I should say that there is one rather obscure situation where Ombudsmen might have the temerity to question merits and that is if we feel the decision was so unreasonable that no reasonable body of Councillors could possibly have come to such a conclusion. This is applying by analogy 'Wednesbury' principles of reasonableness.[3]

Subject to that, why I ask, are 'merits' issues generally out? The answer usually given is that in a democratic system, decisions are made by the Councillors who vote in favour of the proposition and it would be intolerable that an appointed official such as an Ombudsman should be able to overturn the elected representatives. This is a valid argument but is it a correct view? For example disappointed applicants for planning permission can appeal the local planning authority's decision. The appeal is heard by an inspector appointed by the Secretary of State, but undisputedly an appointed official. He can and often does overturn the Council's decision, and so where is the logical distinction between that situation and empowering the Local Ombudsman to say that, for good reasons, any other decision is unfair, it caused injustice and should be reviewed?

Remedies

As you will know the Commissioners are paper tigers, they have no sanction to enforce their recommendations. This is viewed with alarm from time to time and the policy of my Commission is to seek a legal sanction for their reports. The Commission favours the system now available in Northern Ireland where a disappointed complainant can go to the County Court to seek an order compelling the recalcitrant Council to provide the remedy proposed by the Ombudsmen. That is my Commission's policy but I view that change with some anxiety because the Ombudsman system is characterised by informality and depends on good relations with local authorities. To attach a legal remedy would undermine the way in which the system presently works and would inevitably raise barriers between Ombudsmen and local authorities.

The problem also needs to be put in perspective. As at the end of 1991 there were only 185 cases since 1974 when the Ombudsmen's recommended remedies had not been provided in whole or part - a very small number measured against the reports issued which presently run at 300 or more per annum.

3 *Associated Provincial Picture Houses Ltd. v. Wednesbury Corporation* (1948) 1 KB 123.

Ombudsmen around the world

The Ombudsman system is a growth industry and is world wide. There is expansion even into the former empire of the Soviet Union. We have seen a dramatic growth in this country since 1968 and there are now other statutory Ombudsmen in the fields of banking, building societies and pensions and other Ombudsmen of equal status in the insurance and other industries. I am becoming concerned about further confusing the public by the proliferation because John and Jill Citizen think in terms of the Ombudsman, not a multiple of officers. Each of the main political parties is proposing some kind of Citizen Charter to enhance customer care, accountability of service providers and promote better quality.

The Charter seems to me to be vague as to the value of the supervisory body. The Government's proposals advocate 'lay adjudicators'. The Labour Party want other Ombudsmen and the Liberal Democrats want to enhance the role and powers of existing Ombudsmen.

I am quite astonished by some politicians' pronouncements about the need for Ombudsmen because they seem to overlook the present incumbents' existence. We hear of a Children's Ombudsman and an Education Ombudsman when in fact, with the limitations I have referred to, I already work in those service areas.

My theme therefore is that there are inefficiencies and pitfalls in appointing Ombudsmen over liberally. Do we really need them at all? Could we have in fact one all-embracing Ombudsman? That may be a tall order but standard complaint investigating techniques could apply to any subject matter. My Commission does not go out of its way to appoint specialists to deal with complaints within that specialism. We look for investigators with bright minds, a will and ability to sieve through the story and establish the facts on which a judgment can be made. If the judgment needs specialist guidance then it can be taken but a complaint is a complaint whatever the subject.

Conclusion

Having served as a Commissioner for seven years I am convinced of the value of the Ombudsmen's service as an inexpensive means of examining grievances. As I have suggested the service could be improved and extended to meet the needs of a society who seem dedicated to complaining.